The Storytelling School

Handbook for Teachers

Chris Smith PhD & Adam Guillain
Foreword by Pie Corbett

Storytelling Schools Series
Volume I

Second Edition

storytelling schools
where every child is a storyteller

Hawthorn Press

Hawthorn Press

Published by Hawthorn Press, Hawthorn House,

1 Lansdown Lane, Stroud, Gloucestershire, GL5 1BJ, UK

Tel: (01453) 757040

E-mail: info@hawthornpress.com

Website: www.hawthornpress.com

UK Edition *The Storytelling School Handbook for Teachers* © Hawthorn Press 2014

First Edition by the Story Museum

Cover illustration © Shirin Adl

Illustrations by Shirin Adl

Cover design and typesetting by Lucy Guenot

Printed by Berforts Information Press Ltd, Herts, UK

Reprinted by Henry Ling, The Dorset Press, Dorchester 2018, 2020.

The views expressed in this book are not necessarily those of the publisher.

Printed on environmentally friendly chlorine-free paper manufactured from renewable forest stock.

British Library Cataloguing in Publication Data applied for

ISBN Number 978-1-907359-38-5

About the authors

Chris Smith PhD

Chris Smith, PhD, is a storyteller, educational trainer and founding director of Storytelling Schools. Chris loves helping to make education more joyful, effective and engaging, especially in areas of social deprivation where good education can make such a difference to future life chances. For the last ten years Chris has been researching and developing the Storytelling Schools idea in UK schools. Chris has also been a father, musician, exhibition designer, performer, monk, UN manager, human ecologist, surfer and writer. He currently divides his time between a house in Oxford and a wood in Devon. For more information on Chris see: www.storysmith.co.uk

Adam Guillain

Adam Guillain, BA (Hons) PGCE, is an experienced primary school teacher and educational consultant. He is also widely published in both trade and educational children's fiction and runs creative writing workshops and insets based on the Storytelling Schools model outlined in this handbook. During 2006, Adam was writer-in-residence at the Roald Dahl Museum and Story Centre in Great Missenden and joined the Story Museum outreach team in 2008. For more information on Adam's published work, visit www.tinnedspaghetti.co.uk

Storytelling Schools

Storytelling Schools is a group of educationalists who are passionate about the power of storytelling to transform education and learning. We were founded in 2013 to promote the Storytelling Schools model throughout the UK and beyond. We think by systematically learning storytelling skills at school, students can receive an education that builds confidence and fluency in spoken language and raises standards of reading and writing. Storytelling is also a great way to learn other subjects in the curriculum, all in a way that is engaging, enjoyable and empowering.

Storytelling Schools make information, resources and training available for teachers who wish to adopt this approach in their school.

Our founders are Chris Smith, Adam Guillain, Pie Corbett and Nanette Stormont.

For more information see our website at **www.storytellingschools.com**

Acknowledgements

Deep appreciation for our brilliant colleague Nanette Stormont for her insightful and invaluable input into this volume.

I (Chris) would like to honour three of my teachers: Ben Haggarty, who taught me about performance and storytelling; Alida Gersie, who opened the door to the world of stories and group-work; and finally the wonderful Pie Corbett. Although Pie was never formally my teacher I learned a huge amount about education by working alongside him over several years. The content of this handbook reflects these three areas of learning: performative, therapeutic and educational.

Secondly, I am indebted to the many schools which have offered time, resources and expertise to put the storytelling idea into practice. It has been an honour to work with these schools, and be invited into the frontline world of city estate education, where inspiring teaching can really make a difference. In particular I am grateful to the support of Jill Hudson, headteacher at the excellent Pegasus Primary School in Blackbird Leys, Oxford, for supporting and inspiring this work over several years and to Sue Mortimer, headteacher at Rose Hill Primary, for her ongoing support and encouragement.

Two excellent teachers were important in developing and testing many of these ideas: Beth Wooldridge at SS Mary and John CE Primary School and Nanette Stormont at Pegasus Primary School.

Schools where these models have been explored and developed include:

Bayards Hill Primary School, Barton, Oxford

Bishop Loveday CE Primary School, Banbury

Bodicote Primary School, Banbury

East Oxford Primary School, East Oxford

SS Mary and John CE Primary School, East Oxford

St John Fisher Catholic Primary School, Littlemore, Oxford

Orchard Meadow Primary School, Blackbird Leys, Oxford

Our Lady's Catholic Primary School, Cowley, East Oxford

Pegasus Primary School, Blackbird Leys, Oxford

Rose Hill Primary School, Rose Hill, Oxford

Watlington Primary School, Watlington

Windale Community Primary School, Blackbird Leys, Oxford

Wood Farm Primary School, Wood Farm, Headington, Oxford

The Storytelling Schools programme was developed with the support of The Story Museum and the generosity of its funders and volunteers. The Story Museum is a charity dedicated to exploring and celebrating the power of story to inspire learning and enrich lives, especially young lives. It runs outreach programmes in schools and communities and is building a magical centre of stories in the heart of Oxford. Visit **www.storymuseum.org.uk** for details of its exhibition, event and learning programmes.

The authors would especially like to thank Emily Hunter, Jane Glennie, Jackie Fortey, the Story Museum team and SHINE for their help in creating and publishing the first edition. Thanks also to Shirin Adl for her wonderful illustrations.

For this second edition, thanks to Martin, Claire and Lucy at Hawthorn Press for their support, enthusiasm and invaluable help in creating this volume.

Contents

Foreword by Pie Corbett   vii

Preface   xii

Chapter 1
Introduction   1
What's the main idea?   1
How was the idea developed?   3
What are the benefits?   3
Key features of the Storytelling School   7
What is in the rest of this handbook?   9

Chapter 2
How to learn a story and tell it to your class   11
Learning the technique   11
Choosing a story   11
How to prepare with HMSS   14
Tips for telling to your class   18
Types of story and how to tell them   20
Some ways to refine and develop your story   22

Chapter 3
Games and warm-ups   25
Storytelling 'starters'   25
Questioning games   26
Reflection and copying games   30
Conversation and dialogue games   32
Whole group re-enactment   33
Guessing games   33
Storymaking games   34

Chapter 4
How to teach a story to your class   35
Hear, Map, Step, Speak   35
Method and key principles   35
1. Hear   36
2. Map   36
3. Step   38
4. Speak   43
Giving feedback after storytelling   44

Chapter 5
Deepening   47
Growing new stories   47
Deepening exercises   47
Introducing basic plots and characters   52

Chapter 6
Innovation   57
What is innovation?   57
Changing stories   57
How to teach innovation   59

Chapter 7
Invention   61
Creating new stories   61
What is invention?   61
'Spontaneous' invention   63
Invention from a basic plot   63
Invention from a character   66
Invention with objects   69
Using the plot matrix   70
Believability   73
Conclusion   75

Chapter 8
Shared writing — 77

Turning oral into written stories — 77
Key principles — 77
Three ways to demonstrate writing — 81
Shared writing — 81
Shared editing — 82
Unilateral demonstration modelling — 82
Examples of shared writing sessions — 83
Examples of shared editing — 89
Example of unilateral demonstration — 91
Example of teaching specific language features — 91
Example of adaptations for KS1 — 92
Thinking like a writer — 93
Teachers as writers — 93

Chapter 9
Non-fiction: Six types of communication — 94

Introduction — 94
Why do they matter? — 95
Similarities to fiction teaching — 96
Differences from fiction teaching — 96
Warm-ups — 99
Sequencing your non-fiction teaching — 103
Imitation — 103
Innovation — 108
Invention — 109
Shared and independent writing — 109

Chapter 10
Curriculum integration — 115

Introduction — 115
Literacy — 116
History — 128
Personal and Social Education — 133
Religion — 140
Science — 142
Music — 144

Chapter 11
Making it happen — 145

Becoming a Storytelling School — 145
Diversity is the spice of life — 145
School leadership — 146
Launching the initial policy — 146
Building up the skills step by step — 147
Including teaching support staff — 148
Parents — 148
Celebration and visibility — 148
Planning stories into the curriculum — 149
Induction of new staff — 149
Support networks — 150
Falling in love with a story — 150
Afterword — 150

Sources and resources — 155

Further reading — 157

Index — 162

Stories

The Three Dolls — xiv
The Freedom Song — 12
Anansi and the Tiger — 55
Otto Frank — 129
The Great Fire of London — 130
Icarus — 134
Snip-snip — 137
Nativity Chant — 141
Benjamin Franklin's Kite — 142
Monkeys and Hats — 152

Foreword

The story of Storytelling Schools

Stories are magical. Every teacher knows that. You read or tell a story. Silence descends. Children stare at you, through you and into a world beyond, and yet inside of them. In this inner world, the story is recreated. Indeed, the telling can be so powerful that a story may make us laugh, feel afraid or even cry. Quite often when I tell a story, children ask, 'was that real?' and in a way, yes it was.

Gordon Wells' research showed that children who are read to in the first four years of their lives are the most likely to succeed in education. This is because constant engagement with stories develops the ability to sit, listen and concentrate. It builds a child's imaginative world, littering the mind with characters, settings and possibilities. These are the building blocks that they will need when they come to create their own stories. You cannot create out of nothing.

Stories also provide children with vocabulary, the elegant turn of phrase, the tune of well-written prose. All of this will be reflected into children's writing. The richness and depth of story experience shapes and determines the writer a child becomes. Reading creates our written style. Children who have been read to and who read avidly are the first to form abstract concepts across the curriculum, for the imagination develops the ability to think in the abstract. So, story helps to make you brainy!

Stories pass on culture, broadening our sense of world culture – for many stories are similar from one place to another. We may look different but we are just human beings. It also provides us with that inner template that helps us to understand

ourselves and the world we inhabit. Narrative is what helps us begin to understand human existence. We reach for it to help us cope with the incomprehensible. Without the ability to take the chaos of our lives and create, we become destructive. Illiteracy is the fist of destruction.

About 40 years ago, I began to tell stories as part of my teaching repertoire. Over the years, my bank of stories steadily grew. They became my faithful travelling companions. I had noticed that the best writers were always readers. I knew that somehow constant reading was building children's imagination but also providing them with elegant ways of expressing their ideas. Indeed, if you looked carefully at a child's writing, you could often tell which author they were reading. The writing reflected the reading.

Gradually, over many years, I learned that many children might struggle with reading but could retell a well-known story. When I was working in teacher training, the storyteller Ben Haggarty worked with my students for several days. Ben and I discussed how young children learned by imitating. This linked to all that I knew about early learning – children copy. This simple notion began to develop into a specific stage of learning that I called 'imitation'. Children's early language development is based on 'copying' the words, phrases and expressions that they hear at home.

I knew too that small children pass through a phase where they want to have the same story again and again. This is so common an experience that it must have significance in both language and cognitive development. Why do children want the pattern of a well-loved tale retold so many times that they end up knowing the story word for word? Perhaps it is part of the brain's very real need for the narrative pattern to help us comprehend the world.

Gradually I realised that it is not so much the book that mattered but the story. Indeed, one teacher pointed out to me that she had been brought up in Ghana where there were no books but her grandmother told stories. She could remember passing through the stage of demanding the same story again and again – and she could still recall all her grandmother's stories, passed on orally. Of course, reading books matters but why does the oral tale matter so much?

From the teacher's angle, telling a story without the book means that you can directly engage with the children, drawing them into the tale, scanning round the class. This direct intimacy is a very powerful strategy for ensuring that almost every child becomes rapidly involved in the story's spell. As many teachers who start storytelling comment – the book 'gets in the way'.

As you are telling the story, it is easier to hold the class. If you have learned a story orally from a storyteller then, initially, the rhythm and pattern of the tale will be very similar to the version that you learned. It is almost as if the storyteller's voice is coming out of your mouth. Teachers comment that 'when I tell the story I keep hearing your voice'. However, after a few tellings the voice of the original teller recedes and the story becomes your own.

Because the teacher is facing the children, it is easier to read their emotions. A cruel moment may be lightened, pace picked up, an event savoured, a dramatic pause used. The way in which the children listen helps to shape the actual telling of the tale. It is almost as if the telling is actually a double act with the listener contributing as much as the teller. So through telling stories in the classroom, I began to learn that telling was different to story reading and had a very powerful effect on children.

As soon as I began to get children to tell stories, I realised there were other advantages. I noticed that many children who carried the unhelpful label 'special needs' had a real talent for telling stories. Here was something that they could do – there was no barrier of reading or writing. Many of these children had had to become quite skillful orally. Some were renowned for being too chatty and had a certain verbal dexterity. They were funny, upfront and not afraid to tell stories. This gave them success.

With younger children, I experimented with using picture books. It soon became clear to me that if the children learned the story orally then they would all be able to read the text. Now, of course, this idea seems very obvious. The technique gave children confidence in reading and meant everyone could have access to a class story. Whilst I have little tangible proof for this, I would be willing to bet good money that learning stories improves reading – because the children are learning the syntactical patterns that they meet in reading and will therefore be more likely to spot these as they read books.

As I developed my storytelling work in classrooms, I realised too that if a story was developed orally, as a precursor to writing, it made the actual act of writing easier. I noticed that some children would shift from only writing a few lines to suddenly writing pages. Why would this be so? Well, if the composition is well developed then the children are more motivated to try with their writing. They have a story to tell. Secondly, the act of writing has been made easier. The composition (the actual flow of sentences) is already well-known. They have retold and refined their version of the story (oral revision is so much easier for a young child). So, the story is developed, the child is motivated. As they settle down to write, the children can put their effort into making sure that the spelling and punctuation are accurate – and the handwriting neat. The process splits the act of writing so that the composition is developed before the transcription. Most children are trying to accomplish both at once – and if you find spelling difficult, it is no wonder that children give up!

Another key aspect of telling stories that is worth every teacher knowing about is that the very act of listening to and then retelling a story has a dramatic effect on children's vocabulary and sentence structure. Teachers of younger children often report that they have heard the words from different stories being recycled in children's everyday play and chatter. It is a more rapid and effective way of developing vocabulary and sentence structure than being read to by a teacher. Of course, this is because the children have to say the words themselves so the words and patterns are more likely to stay within the child as part of their linguistic competency.

So, storytelling is a prime strategy for learning language. Vocabulary lists do not work well – retelling a tale and working with it almost guarantees language development. The approach is ideal for children who are new to the English language as well as those who have had a paucity of interactive conversation at home. It is ideal for those who love reading as they can tackle some of the great tales, from *Beowulf* to *The Odyssey*. *Story* develops a confidence in understanding and communicating that all humans need. Furthermore, the power of a Storytelling School is that children build their vocabulary, sentence structure and plot patterns over many years. It is the cumulative effect that ultimately releases linguistic story power.

Over the years, I realised that working with a story and processing it in many ways – through art, dance, music, discussion, mapping, drama – helped children understand a story, inhabit its world and take it to heart forever. Constantly skipping from one picture book to another passed the time of day but did not have such an effect. It is worth loitering with stories so that they become part of the child's linguistic repertoire as well as their metaphorical world.

I also noticed that oral storytelling helped children's behaviour. The very nature of telling stories together, working in groups or pairs to develop a tale brought children together into cooperative learning. The satisfaction of having a story and the very real sense of accomplishment and pleasure when an audience reacts is a great motivator and builder of self esteem. Reading stories is a somewhat isolated activity.

A storytelling classroom is very cooperative. Story binds us together as a community of tellers.

A few years on and I was working on the National Literacy Strategy. I helped to create the notion of 'Grammar for Writing'. This ended up as a book for every primary school as well as training for teachers across the country. My experience as a writer informed a view of grammar as a skill – the ability to choose the right word, to construct and vary sentences creating different effects and then tying the text together. This work moved grammar on from being just about 'knowledge' into grammar becoming an important aspect of writing. Children learned their grammar through engaging as a writer. This work sharpened the profession's understanding of language and how it worked.

In the year 2000, I was writing a 'flyer' for the National Literacy Strategy about teaching story writing. I knew that it was helpful if children started with what we might describe as a 'model' story. This would be told and retold, read and discussed but also dramatised, scenes painted and models made until the children knew the story really well. It was rather like feeding the brain with a story by retelling and reprocessing it many ways so that the children almost become characters within the story. I called this stage 'Imitation'.

I also knew that it was helpful for young children to 'innovate' on known stories. Ted Hughes described myths as being rather like 'blueprints for the imagination'. A known story could be altered or embellished to create something new. Many storytellers and teachers worked in this way so that children would be taught a story and in the retelling perhaps make it their own by adding their own local flavour. I called this stage 'Innovation'.

Now, I also knew that it was important for children to make up their own stories. This seemed to me a very natural part of play and daydreaming. Children (indeed, adults too) are constantly retelling the story of what has happened to them as well as creating the story of what might happen next. When my own children were very young, they spent hours playing with little toys and 'pretending'. This story making seemed to be very natural and satisfying. They would interweave aspects of stories that they knew, picture books, characters from rhymes as well as their own life in a tumble of images and ideas often accompanied by much laughter and joy.

This ability to make stories up I called 'Invention'. I can remember the actual moment that the word came to me because I had 'imitation' and 'innovation' and I wanted the third stage of 'making one up' to start in the same way and – bingo! The word 'invention' appeared with a sudden rush of surprise. It seemed a perfect way to describe the story process – 'imitation, innovation, invention'.

We feed the mind with stories, rhymes and non-fiction. This builds our inner bank of ideas, images and language patterns. Then we need the ability to manipulate those patterns to create new tales. Finally, in order to invent a totally new story, we draw upon our inner store and imagination to create something new. Since that moment, I have been lucky enough to work with large numbers of teachers and schools developing this simple-sounding framework.

David Almond (author of *Skellig*) and I completed that original flyer, providing advice for teachers and young writers. It was built around the three 'I's. David drew on his teaching experience as well as his writing to help develop

the notion of a story cycle – how the reading and retelling informs the writing and performing. At the International Learning and Research Centre I was lucky enough to co-lead, with Mary Rose, a storymaking project where we took this notion further forwards as we investigated learning a second language through storymaking. Children learned stories in their home language and then the same tale in a new language. The Department for Education then funded several further years of teacher research into the links between learning stories orally and then innovating on them to improve writing.

Since then, thousands of teachers have experimented with these basic ideas, developing and refining new strategies and approaches. Speech therapists deepened my understanding of the innovation stage by pointing out that this was really based on generative grammar. Generative grammar is the brain's extraordinary ability to extract the underlying structures of a language, which can then be used to create new utterances. This idea helped us to develop key sentence patterns and story language that might be repeated cumulatively, for children learn language by memorable, meaningful repetition – primarily by hearing and saying.

Shared writing has always been central to my teaching and was an important aspect of my work as a writer in many schools. The simple notion that teaching any form of writing hinged around 'doing one together' seemed obvious to me. As a young poet, I was lucky to be asked to visit other schools and run writing workshops. I soon discovered that the large majority of teachers did not use shared writing and even today there is still a lack of confidence in engaging children in creating together.

The National Literacy Trust (and the Basic Skills Agency) encouraged and supported all of this work, providing me with an opportunity to share my thinking with thousands of teachers. I was fortunate enough to work with Julia Strong from the Trust who has now been developing this work, focusing on 'talk for writing across the curriculum' in secondary schools. In 2006, the National Primary Strategy asked me to lead a project with teachers and consultants across the country, developing what became known as 'Talk for Writing'. Ultimately, this led into every consultant being trained, as well as materials for every primary school and training for thousands of teachers.

The Department for Education then asked me to investigate the role of 'Teachers and Teaching Assistants as Writers'. This project focused on using shared writing and led into a further project, establishing 30 'Writing Schools' across the country. These schools went on to train others, sharing expertise.

Around this time I visited Trevithick Primary School in Cornwall. In every classroom, I saw story maps, role-play areas and shared writing. Story was central to the lifeblood of the school. Here was a school that made sure that children would learn a bank of tales, with daily storytelling to enrich the children's lives. The school is in a challenging area, in the bottom 3% on the socio-economic scale. When Sean Powers, the Head, arrived in 2006, the children achieved 34% level 4. In the last 3 years they have achieved over 90% level 4 and this year 55% level 5 in writing. Sean, and his deputy Kaye, have transformed the teachers into story teachers and they in turn have transformed the life chances of the children. Isn't that what education should do?

I was moved to see how the school had story at its heart. Children read stories, told stories, invented stories, dramatised them – story was becoming the vehicle which was raising standards and developing creativity. Story was letting the imagination loose. Moved, and without quite knowing what I was saying, I told Sean that his was the first 'Storytelling School' in the country. On the train back, I imagined that we might have thousands of storytelling schools across our country and round the world.

I recently went back. They have a plaque up on the wall proclaiming their status as the first Storytelling School in the country with 'Pie' approval!

Some of my most memorable teaching has been with Chris and Adam, the authors of this marvellous book. Some mornings Chris has led the way in a school, teaching a story. After break, I have taken this into the classroom and modelled how to begin crafting the innovation using shared writing. There is something in this book that is deep and genuinely educational that is well worth every primary teacher considering. This book sets out the activities that have been developed so far. Over the next few years, we will all learn more about how we help children develop their story and how we create Storytelling Schools. New editions and other support materials will be developed.

Every culture around the world has at its heart stories. If our classrooms and schools do not have stories at their heart then they are heartless places, dry as dust on the wind. It is story that gives us soul and gives our spirit a voice. May this book help to create Storytelling Schools across this country and indeed around the world.

Pie Corbett

Preface

Have you ever wondered why most young children love listening to spoken stories? Why they will sit for hours, spellbound, fully captivated, absorbing story after story? Why they will ask for the same story again and again? Why they love joining in and, when ready, delight in making up their own versions?

Our minds are hard-wired for stories. Long before there were schools, long before there was writing, our species was telling and retelling stories as a way of passing on knowledge and skills to each new generation. Just as we are programmed to eat, bond and protect our families, so our survival has depended on parents passing skills of thinking, sequencing and remembering to their children, often through the medium of stories.

If you have spent much time in pre-school centres, you may have noticed that, by the age of four, some children are happily and confidently chattering away using complex sentences and abstract ideas, while others have not yet mastered a basic sentence. Often the more articulate children come from homes that are rich in story and language. Their parents have been filling them up with words and tales since the day they were born. For a couple of years, they soak up the words like sponges and then, in that wonderful miracle of child development, they start to use the words themselves. If their speech is celebrated, encouraged and rewarded by their carers, then they are likely to develop into confident speakers, ready and eager to use their words to engage with the wider world by the time they start school.

Conversely, in families where there is not so much time for conversation and story-sharing, a child will not have the same opportunity to learn. By the age of four, such children can be more than two years behind their more advantaged peers. They may have absorbed a certain amount of passive vocabulary from electronic sources, but will have had relatively little support in the active use of language in speech (i.e. talking with someone who is listening, coaching and encouraging them).

Now let's follow the students through school. Some come home every day and talk about their school day, with conversations over supper, bedtime stories, and parents eager to buy books to improve their child's language. Others will be struggling to keep up, maybe having some extra help with reading at school but getting much less language practice at home. Parents or carers may be too busy, too stressed, may have rudimentary language skills themselves, or they may simply not know how crucial their verbal interactions are to their child's future.

I remember the last time I bought a car (after my last one had been stolen and burned by a couple of young lads who had dropped out of the local school). The salesman who sold me my new car had recently become a father for the first time. 'Congratulations!' I said. 'Are you telling him stories yet?' 'Oh no,' said the salesman, 'no need. He can't talk yet.'

Fast-forward a few years. Some students are getting ready for GCSEs with a mind full of skills and words and ideas that can be used with confidence in the exams. These students made the transition from speaking and listening to reading and writing, building on their confidence and enjoyment of language. Some others struggled to keep up and have already mentally left school. They never really managed to engage with the content of their education because their lack of language skills hindered their reading, writing and learning.

Our friend and mentor Pie Corbett tells the story of when he was a teacher in Tulse Hill, then a tough area of South London. He remembers watching an argument between two teenage boys. One was an articulate boy, laying into a less articulate boy with a torrent of words and arguments about why he was right. The less articulate one opened his mouth to speak but no words would come. There was just silence, met by a sneer. He didn't have the words to fight back with. Instead his hand turned into a fist.

Pie had to break up the fight.

We're not saying that everyone should be speaking posh Oxford English. The point is simply that most people would agree that in order to navigate our way through life successfully in the 21st century, good enough skills in speaking, listening, reading and writing are crucial. In the sphere of work, good communication skills are usually a must, at the stage of interview and then in relationships with others in the workplace. In the personal sphere, if we struggle with words we may struggle with our relationships, unable to say what needs to be said. As for reading and writing … well it's obvious isn't it?

So, rather than flog a dead horse, let's just say that language development is a crucial life skill, and that students who grow up in a story-rich environment tend to develop better skills in communication and understanding of various kinds, compared to their peers from a less story-rich environment. While all this is probably pretty obvious to anyone working in primary education in a disadvantaged area, it's less obvious what to do about it: despite all the government programmes, it is notoriously difficult to affect the home language environment of a child. Most vulnerable families tend to be the hardest to reach.

So, if we want to level out the playing field, if we want to give every child a fair chance to achieve their potential, if we want a society of more articulate and imaginative communicators, then we need ways of teaching that help those from poorer language environments to catch up before they drop out, while allowing more advanced students to develop their language, communication and creative potential further.

The Storytelling School offers you one way to do this. In a Storytelling School all pupils learn to be storytellers, which is a great thing for all students regardless of ability or background. Storytelling can make learning a pleasure, developing skills in speaking and listening, confidence, creativity and empathy, while providing a great springboard for writing and storymaking. So it's not just about helping students who are falling behind. It's a way for all students to fulfil their potential, both within the education system, both primary and secondary, and in the wider world. This book will tell you how to make it happen in your school.

Benefits include:

✓ accelerated language learning

✓ increased inclusion and engagement

✓ enlivened teaching across the whole curriculum

✓ creation of memorable moments of magic in the classroom

✓ strengthened core life skills of speaking and sequencing from memory

✓ improved self-esteem and enjoyment for both staff and students

The Three Dolls

Once there was a school where the teacher was thought to be very wise. In all his classes the students listened to his wise words and tried to remember them and in the exams would try to write them down. Some did well and some did not so well, but everyone agreed that everything the teacher said was very wise.

One day the teacher issued a challenge to his class.

'I challenge you all to set me a riddle that I cannot answer. If you succeed, then make a wish and if I can, I will grant it.'

The next day the students tried their riddles.

'What has hands and a face but no heart?'

'What has a bed and runs all day but has no feet?'

'What has a head and foot and four legs but no tummy?'

And so on...

The teacher guessed them all easily – a clock, a river, a bed – until the daughter of the village storyteller (a troublesome and rather noisy girl) gave him three wooden dolls.

'Tell me teacher, what's the difference between the three dolls?'

He looked and looked but they all seemed the same.

'I need time,' he said.

That playtime he asked the smartest child in the school into his office.

'Can you tell the difference between these dolls?' he said.

She smelled and weighed and measured and touched and just shrugged.

'No idea!'

Then he asked the most foolish child in the school.

He just played with them and laughed.

'Look teacher, it is obvious. These two are in love, and this one is a space rocket!'

After playtime the teacher admitted defeat.

'I can't tell the difference!' he said. 'What's the answer?'

The storyteller's daughter plucked a white hair from his wise beard and stuck it into the ear of the first doll. The hair went in and did not come out anywhere else.

'This first one is what you call a good student. Everything he hears goes in and stays in and he remembers it. In the exams he writes it down. This is the meaning of this doll.'

Next, she stuck the hair into the ear of the second doll. This time the end of the hair came out of the other ear.

'This is what you call the bad student. He remembers nothing. What goes in one ear comes out the other. This one fails the exams.'

Finally, she put the hair into the ear of the third doll. Its end came out of the doll's mouth, this time with a little curl on the end. She grinned.

'This one is the storytelling student – it all goes in the ear and comes out of the mouth. See how the hair is twisted. It is a little different when it comes out. The storytelling student can listen, remember and then retell the story in his own way.'

'And here is the thing teacher, the clever doll will do well in exams, but the storyteller student will do well in life. Which is the most important to you?'

'Very interesting,' said the teacher. 'I admit defeat. What is your wish?'

'Teach us all to be storytellers!' she said.

From that day, instead of just telling the stories, he taught all his pupils to listen and retell stories in their own way. Soon their exam results went up and the students learned all sorts of amazing things that prepared them for life after school.

That's how the first Storytelling School began.

Adapted from a telling by David Novak.

Chapter 1

Introduction

What's the main idea?

In a Storytelling School students learn to tell stories from memory, not as a one-off, but as a systematic approach to teaching and learning throughout the whole of their stay in the school. By 'storytelling' here, we mean one person speaking a story to an audience of at least one other person, the story being told from memory (not read from a book).

The core principle in this approach is that telling stories is a great way to learn about language, communication and ideas. Listening to stories fills the listener up with words, but learning to tell that same story moves those words and phrases from the passive to the active language part of the brain; the new elements of language become ready to be used. It is a bit like riding a bike: it is one thing to watch someone riding and get the general idea, and quite another to learn to ride it yourself. In this way, storytelling internalises patterns of language and plot that the storyteller will then be able to use actively, both in speaking and later in writing.

The act of learning to speak a story also creates a deeper identification with the content of the story than is possible by just reading or memorising from a text. To tell a story well, you have to know the characters, setting and plot intimately.

In a Storytelling School, the teacher can introduce a range of different topics by telling a relevant story to their class.

This could be:

➤ a traditional tale;

➤ a biographical tale;

➤ a historical tale;

➤ any narrative that can be told as an interesting and engaging story.

After the telling, the students will use a series of simple and efficient techniques to learn and then retell the story a few times in their own words, so that the language and content of the story is fully internalised. From there the teacher has many options for ways of working with the learned story that may involve a combination of deepening activities, innovations or writing exercises of one kind or another.

The approach begins at Foundation Stage (3 years and up) and continues through to the end of Key Stage 2 (11 years old). During this period the students become experts at listening, remembering and retelling and are able to apply those skills to many aspects of their learning. They also graduate with a mind full of wonderful stories and the confidence to share them with others.

Obviously in a Storytelling School there needs to be a certain amount of planning and training. Usually literacy coordinators, or story coordinators, work with storytellers to develop the school's story curriculum, choosing a series of stories to be learned in each year group creating a model something like this:

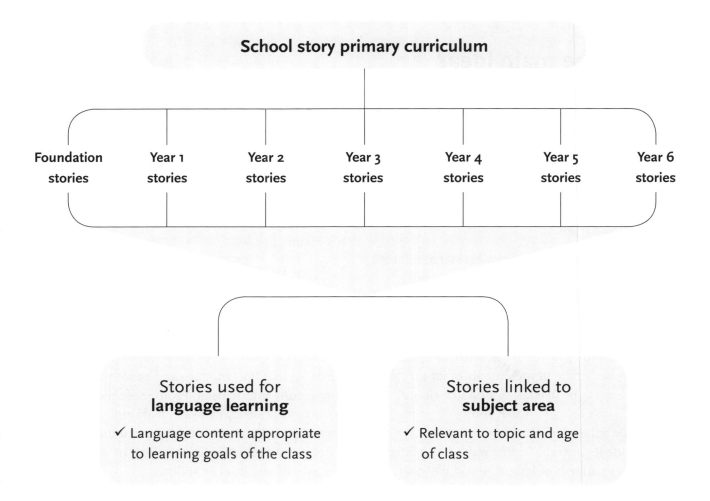

In all cases though, the main thing is to find great narratives – interesting and engaging tales that are easy to tell and which students will love. A minimum of 15 minutes per day or an equivalent time per week is allocated for storytelling in these schools.

As for training, it is crucial that all teaching staff are fluent with the basic methods of teaching storytelling. All teachers and teaching assistants need to be able to prepare and retell stories to their class efficiently from memory and teach students to do the same.

They need to be able to work from a learned story to a wide range of curriculum tasks that include:

➤ Drama
➤ Writing
➤ Reading
➤ Art
➤ History and geography
➤ Science
➤ Religious education
➤ Personal, Social and Health Education.

How was the idea developed?

The Storytelling School mixes three things: the retelling of stories, drama techniques and creative writing. There is nothing new in mixing these three areas. Archival research shows that programmes aimed at promoting functional literacy have combined these three elements for at least 100 years, both in North America and Europe.

In general, however, such programmes have not been at the heart of primary education: rather, storytelling within schools has been seen as an add-on, an enrichment activity or a discrete subject to be covered when looking at traditional tales. What is revolutionary about this method is that it changes the basic way in which that learning occurs.

The Storytelling School idea itself originated with Pie Corbett who, in early 2003, was co-leading a pilot research project into ways of teaching a second language. They discovered that using a storytelling method was fast, efficient and effective. Students who learned to retell tales in a foreign language quickly got the hang of speaking and using the new words and phrases. They then tried applying the same method to the learning of English in schools, using the same principles, and discovered that it was equally effective.

At first storytelling was seen as a tool to accelerate the learning of English, but over time the concept evolved into the idea of a Storytelling School, where all students learn to tell stories from memory as a core strategy for learning language. Many of Pie's ideas were central to the 2006 'Talk for Writing' initiative of the English government, where storytelling was emphasised as a way to improve standards in writing.

Since 2007 we have been working with Pie on three main research projects. Schools have signed up to the idea of becoming a Storytelling School and have received a series of training programmes together with regular visits and monitoring from our training team. We worked first in five schools in various parts of Oxfordshire. Then we formed a partnership with two clusters of schools in the most disadvantaged parts of Oxford City, where indices of deprivation were in the UK's bottom 10%. The projects lasted between two and four years. This handbook is based on the results of these pilot projects.

What are the benefits?

Writing

Many schools in England are under huge pressure to improve their standards in writing, not only because this is important, but also because it is one of the targets around which the government monitors and intervenes.

In a Storytelling School, standards of writing will improve. Students begin to gather together the language of stories from the nursery onwards, so will be able to draw on an ever-growing repertoire of language patterns which they have not just heard but have actively mastered in improvised speech. This knowledge of words and how to string them together into narratives is a basic prerequisite for fluent writing. Choice of good, exciting stories and the use of kinaesthetic ways of retelling them also includes learners who might otherwise be reluctant.

In addition, students will have positive experiences of sharing their stories orally with others, and this can then be continued into the writing sphere. Students who develop pride and enthusiasm for their story ideas can also be motivated to get the ideas down onto paper so that they can be shared and enjoyed by others in the written form.

Listening

If speaking was more important than listening we would have two tongues and one ear!

Listening to others is hugely important in all walks of life. It is one thing to listen to the TV and quite another to listen to a human being in person. In a successful Storytelling School, good listening, human-to-human, is key. In a Storytelling School listening can be a joy, a pleasure, a wonderful thing to do.

How do we make listening memorable and enjoyable? There are many ways of doing this. Most schools use a mixture of playful games to help develop active listening. These games incorporate response tasks for listeners so that students' listening has purpose and focus. Of course, whenever there is magic in the storytelling then the audience will listen, simply because it is wonderful to do so. Because the listeners will be storytellers themselves, they will also be keen to 'magpie' (steal) good ideas from

others to put into their own stories. All of this becomes a habit with time and needs a certain amount of skill, energy and perseverance to establish in a class where listening is weak.

Good active listening is a crucial skill for life in work, in play, in relating to others and, of course, in learning. In almost any sphere of life, the ability to sustain person-to-person listening is critical: husbands listening to wives, parents listening to children, employees listening to bosses, friends listening to problems. Listening makes the world go round.

Empathy

Empathy requires a particularly important kind of listening because we are putting ourselves into the shoes of others, connecting to how they may feel and think. It is hugely important in any relationship. It is how we understand others and learn to show that understanding to them.

People who are weak in empathy can have difficulty understanding how their actions impact on others.

Consider a child who bites you if he does not get his own way. Sometimes the child does not realise that his action causes pain – he just wants his own way. Understanding that someone else gets hurts can be key to preventing this situation in the future.

Consider a child who keeps shouting in class. She may not fully understand how shouting impacts on the feeling of others. When she does, she may change.

Consider a husband who does not have the ability to understand how his wife feels. This can make for a tough marriage!

Storytelling is a great way to learn empathy because, in order to tell a story well, you actively have to put yourself in the shoes of the various characters and understand how they feel. A story only works if the characters' feelings are understood and if the listener cares about those feelings. The storyteller's job is to make that happen.

Confidence Pleasure Respect Autonomy Supportiveness Learning Wonder Memory Inquisitiveness Questioning Speech Writing Language Giving Happiness Pride Reading Accelerate Listening Presentations

Speaking

Speaking and listening go together. The stories we learn give us templates to copy and modify as we retell them to others. At first, students may chant a story word-for-word together, enjoying the anonymity and safety of a group, and often with a degree of physicality to aid memory and keep interest. But as soon as they start telling stories independently, they find their own voice, their own choice of words and their own way of doing things.

Storytelling teaches us that everyone is different and that's great, because every story, every time, is different and differently interesting. Stories fill us up with things to say and different ways to say them while being listened to, and constructive feedback helps make the experience of speaking a pleasure.

Speaking can be a crucial step towards writing. It teaches the basics for any form of good communication, structuring and ordering ideas and delivering content in a way that engages and entertains. It uses language patterns that are then reused in writing. For some, the experience of having one's speech enjoyed by listeners can be dramatic and life-changing, especially for those who are unused to such responses. After a taste of such success, most students will want more.

Reading

Our own experience has also indicated that storytelling can have an impact on the reading habits of students. One girl told us that she was nervous about using the school library, worried that she would be teased for being a swot. When storytelling began in the school, stories soon became 'cool', so she felt that going to the library and collecting more stories would be seen as a good thing.

Once storytellers have achieved a particular level of proficiency, they may also find written versions of stories in books (and on the web) and develop them into oral tales, providing motivation for more reading.

Confidence

There is a fairly universal wish for our words and ideas to be received with respect and appreciation. Students whose words are routinely received with criticism and humiliation will often learn to keep quiet or use minimal speech, reducing their chances for language development whether at school or at home. In the Storytelling School, all students get a chance to tell and be received with respect. When a telling gives pleasure, the child will know this from feedback. Storytelling is deeply personal. When a teller realises that their telling is good enough for others to enjoy their stories, it can have a great effect on the basic sense of self-worth.

Many of our students wax lyrical about moments when they have told a story in the class and then again back home with their family and friends, and how empowering and joyful the experience was of being able to do something which was appreciated, enjoyed and valued by people who matter to them. In this way storytelling builds a kind of community, one story at a time. Some students who really struggle to master reading and writing are absolutely brilliant storytellers. For them, storytelling may give a first taste of success that can kick-start the momentum for learning in other areas.

Appreciation

In a storytelling classroom, appreciation is a key skill. Storytellers need to know that their tales are enjoyed and respected, and positive feedback builds a feeling of safety and support.

Some people have little experience of appreciation and much of criticism. They may feel unsafe and vulnerable when offering praise and may struggle to find things to appreciate. For such a student, learning the basics of appreciation is essential to create the right atmosphere for mutual support. In the wider world, appreciating others is an invaluable quality, whether at work, with friends or in the home. It allows the noting and celebration of positives, helping to sustain friendships and a sense of well-being.

Inquisitiveness and questioning

Stories evolve through inquisitiveness, as listeners enquire about plot and character. This process deepens their understanding about what is going on. We facilitate the development of curiosity by learning how to frame useful questions and generate interesting answers, both in groups and when working alone. Such creative questioning is at the heart of many forms of learning and intellectual enquiry. Storytelling offers a playful place to learn and hone this basic technique.

Subject learning

In school we learn all sorts of things about the world: things that have happened in history, things that go on around the world (geography), how things work (science) and what people believe (religions and philosophy). Storytelling is a great way to bring all this to life. If relevant stories are learned, with engaging characters and plots, then students will place themselves imaginatively within the story and so achieve a closer and more engaged relationship with the subject matter.

Memory and sequencing

Learning to remember a sequence of things in a particular order is another important life skill, which is hugely strengthened through storytelling. Students learn techniques to memorise narratives of increasing complexity and length, developing their mental memory muscles as they do so. Whether we are dealing with a set of directions, instructions, preparing a speech for a wedding or presenting an idea to a meeting, it is good to be able to remember what to say, what to do, and in what order. This is a real life skill.

Autonomy

When a student retells a story independently, they do so with their own voice, their own style, in their own words and with their own ways of evoking character and action. It is a personal process. Each storyteller is different and develops a story differently. A successful telling reinforces their sense of their individual approach as being valid and of value. For those who feel stifled by obedience and conformity, storytelling can be a breath of fresh air.

Rehearsals for life

Stories allow us an imaginative experience of events similar to those that we will encounter in life itself. So, for example, students' stories which explore the theme of fear and danger allow the student to have a taste of what fear is like and to feel it directly. Influential child psychologist Bruno Bettelheim has argued that this is vital for child development so that when fear is encountered in real life, the child is already familiar with it.

Stories also give us plot structures that reflect alternative ways of resolving conflicts and dilemmas. People who have worked in primary education may be familiar with the child whose main story source is video war games. The stories that such a child naturally creates mirror the war game genre: battle, death or victory, then another battle at another level. The child will not create other plots until they have been known and absorbed. Access to a good range of stories provides the child with many other options for invention.

Naturally there is more at stake here than creative writing and telling; stories are also templates for how we look at life. Youth workers will also be familiar with the child whose approach to life mirrors the pattern of confrontation and battle in war games.

Role-plays are equally revealing. Take a story about conflict and see what role-play ideas a group of students come up with. Some simply offer orders, refusals and threats, reflecting the stories they have experienced in their own lives. Others demonstrate subtleties of persuasion and compromise. It just depends on the stories that they have internalised already, whether personal, reported fact or fiction.

Wonder and magic

In one of our most successful Storytelling Schools, in an area of acute social deprivation, the head teacher said to me at an initial meeting, 'I want you to bring magic to our school: magic for the teachers, magic for the students, magic for the governors and magic for the parents. We don't have enough magic in our lives.'

Storytelling works because the experience of it is magical, because we love wonderful stories, because it is 'better than work'.

Their experience of story-listening and storytelling was playful and fun, with that tingle of wonder and magic that makes stories so memorable and special.

When teachers bring magic to their classes, they feel wonderful too. When students bring magic home to their parents, the wonder follows them into the home. It is a virtuous circle.

Key features of the Storytelling School

Many things were learned from our experiences working with these schools. Here are some highlights and key features of the system in practice.

Hear, map, step, speak (HMSS)

After trying various schemes, we settled on a four-step model for learning stories as a default for all schools.

The method proved both popular and robust, offering a variety of sensory markers to aid memory and reinforce the inner-imagined sequence of the story. Stepping proved popular with students who enjoyed channelling their energy into a physical action. Stepping can also be a huge amount of fun. It also works well for students with various kinds of special needs.

1 Hear
The teacher tells the story to the class.

2 Map
Each student draws a simple map of the sequence of main events in the story.

3 Step
Students develop their own way of 'stepping' the story, working out a sequence of freeze-frame gestures, words and sounds that summarise the main sequence of events in the story.

4 Speak
Finally, once the stepping is completed, students are ready to practise telling one another the story, confident that they will remember the main steps of the plot and the key moments.

Imitation, innovation, invention

In early 2000, Pie came up with the brilliant formula of the three 'i's – imitation, innovation, invention – to describe a general progression in learning. They are particularly helpful in emphasising the sequence: first we tend to copy, then we start to modify and finally, when we have a measure of mastery, we are able to create original patterns from the ones we have learned. This model is really helpful for understanding how storytelling develops with time.

Basic plots and characters

Some Storytelling Schools have found it useful to teach students basic plot types (rags to riches, defeating the monster, voyage and return...) as well as basic characters (hero, villain, helper...) from Year 1 onwards, so that all students are familiar with these plot standards. They can then draw on this knowledge when inventing new stories.

Conviction

Every teacher's class is an autonomous kingdom. If change is going to happen in a school, then teachers need to be persuaded that it will work. In schools new to the system, it proved essential to run workshops to present the basic theory of the Storytelling School; how it works and why. Only where the teachers are motivated and can be persuaded that it is worth trying, will it be possible to begin the process of change.

Making teachers' lives easier

We needed a method that made teachers' lives easier. Most teachers we worked with were fed up with having too many initiatives dumped upon them from elsewhere, creating more work and more confusion in their busy teaching lives. For the Storytelling School to succeed, teaching has to be made easier and more enjoyable.

This means that there has to be a certain amount of planning and preparation with the school so that the stories which the teachers need are provided for them well in advance. It is not realistic to expect busy teachers to go and find great stories linked to language and topic goals of various kinds by themselves. That needs a storyteller's eye and takes a certain amount of time and experience.

Storytelling Schools usually compile a whole-school storytelling curriculum so that, at the beginning of each year, teachers are given the text of the stories they will be telling and, where possible, a link to an audio source where the stories can be heard. Sometimes a more experienced storyteller can be used to tell the story to the teacher so that they can learn it quickly and retell it in a satisfactory way.

In this way, once the basic method is mastered, teaching becomes simpler, easier and more effective. A generic set of teaching techniques needs to be internalised, and once learned, they can be applied to all of the stories covered in the year. The content varies but the basic method remains the same, the key skill being the sequencing and calibration of activities to meet the needs of the class.

Leadership and support

Leadership is important. When faced with the idea of radically revising existing ways of working, teachers need reassurance that they will not be penalised for, or left unsupported in, adopting these methods. The head teachers have to make it clear that the Storytelling School is a whole-school priority and that time and resources will be allocated to support its adoption.

It is essential to have a staff member assigned for coordinating the adoption of the storytelling approach to provide advice, resources and help as needed, as well as organising annual induction for new staff arriving at the school.

Shared writing

Most schools give priority to moving from storytelling to independent writing. We found that many teachers are unsure how to do this and feel less than confident, both as writers themselves and, accordingly, as teachers of writing. It has been invaluable to demonstrate and to coach teachers in the process of shared writing. Once these skills are in place, the results are impressive.

Fiction and non-fiction

In our Storytelling Schools, teachers extended the use of the storytelling method to non-fiction texts and across the curriculum. Again, by locating engaging stories that match the curriculum, teachers are able to apply the same storytelling and writing techniques to all subject areas.

School level language policy

Many schools were inspired by the idea of a whole-school language policy that sets out a year-by-year sequence of language features (such as a year-by-year grid of connectives) that students are expected to learn. These schemes enable teachers to plan which features are taught when, and to incorporate the features more systematically into the stories that the students learn.

What is in the rest of this handbook?

We will walk you step-by-step through the process of creating a Storytelling School, explaining all the techniques and information you will need to put this idea into practice. Here is a summary:

Chapter 2
How to learn a story and tell it to your class

We explain the basics of how a teacher can quickly learn to be a 'good enough' storyteller, mastering three forms – chants, participative stories and independent telling – with tips on how to prepare your class for memorable sessions.

Chapter 3
How to make use of games and warm-ups

Here we offer a good repertoire of games and warm-ups to use when needed, building trust, playfulness, ease and a sense of enjoyment.

Chapter 4
How to teach a story to your class

We explain the basic methods of teaching your class to remember and retell, with tips and models that you can use to prepare and engage your students as they learn this for the first time.

Chapter 5
How to deepen the story in the imagination

Once a story has been learned, it is good to stay with it for a while, using various activities to deepen and expand your students' connection with the story. In this chapter, we suggest many ways to do this, developing the story's depth of imagination and the verbal expression.

Chapter 6
How to innovate using a known story

Here we explain various techniques for changing a story once it has been learned, adding, removing and modifying the various story elements.

Chapter 7
How to invent new stories

From innovation, we move on to invention, showing how completely new stories can be created.

Chapter 8
How to teach shared writing using a known story

This section explains the basic technique of shared writing and, once a story has been learned, how to move on from the oral version to a written tale.

Chapter 9
How to teach non-fiction

Here, we look at the non-fiction part of the literacy curriculum and show how to teach this using the same methods as for fiction.

Chapter 10
How to integrate storytelling across the curriculum

Here we look at ways of organising and planning your literacy teaching, then discuss how the storytelling method may be applied to history, PSE, Religion, Science and Music.

Chapter 11
How to make it happen

Finally, we look at the management and support systems needed to create and sustain the Storytelling School.

How the Storytelling School elements fit together

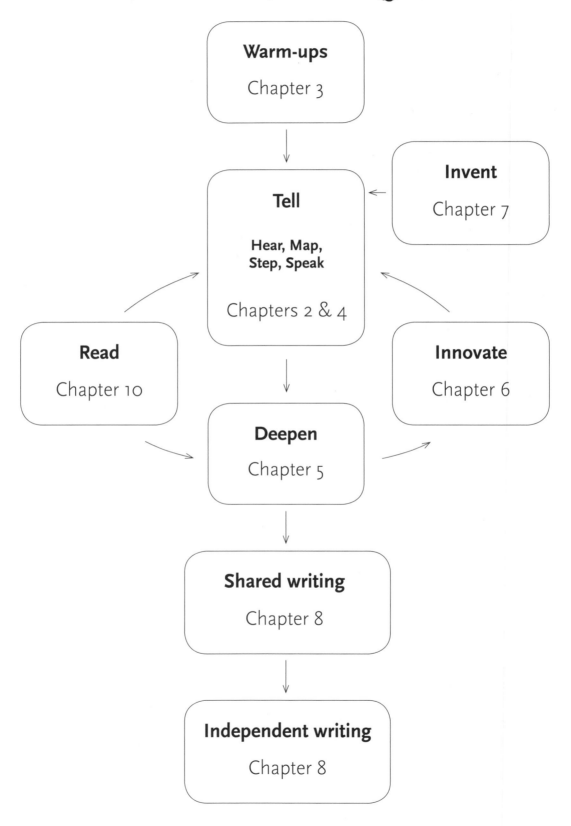

How to learn a story and tell it to your class

Learning the technique

This chapter will get you started with our basic method of learning how to prepare a story for telling to your class. There are four sections within the chapter:

➤ Choosing a story

➤ Preparing the story with *hear, map, step, speak*

➤ Tips for telling to your class

➤ Ways to refine and develop your story

Choosing a story

If you are telling a story for the first time then choose a short story with repeating sections, such as *The Little Red Hen*. Lots of traditional tales are like this. If possible, choose one you really like.

The story also has to be suitable for the age of the students you will be telling it to, although for primary age children most short traditional tales will be fine.

The Story Museum website is a reliable source where you can find more than 100 stories suitable for primary age children, all available as audio files. **www.storymuseum.org.uk/1001stories**

There are three particularly wonderful stories on the Story Museum website that have been tried and tested for beginners. They are *The Freedom Song, Snip-snip*, and *Honey and Trouble*. If in doubt about where to start, you could choose one of these. In this chapter, we will work through the preparation of *The Freedom Song*, an excellent starter story, which was collected by David Holt in Thailand in 1971. You can find his version in *Ready-to-Tell Tales* (see p. 155). Overleaf is our retelling of the tale.

Remember that it will take time to master anything completely. At the start you do not have to be perfect. You may feel nervous; this is quite natural and often makes for a better story, but after a few stories your confidence will grow. With time, your stories will deepen quite naturally. A storytelling teacher does not have to be a virtuoso storyteller, just good enough to get their class interested. The great thing about the HMSS method is that it's really fast and efficient. You will be able to tell a story using this method after less than an hour's work. The more you use it the quicker it becomes. In the end, you can prepare a story in a few minutes.

The Freedom Song

Once there was a hunter. He was a fine hunter. He was a proud hunter. His eyes were sharp and his aim was true. One day he was walking through the forest when he came to a tree. Perched on the top branch of the tree was a bird with a golden beak, a red head, blue wings and a yellow tail.

'What a beautiful bird!' he thought. 'I won't kill it. I'll let it live.'

Just as he was walking away from the tree, the bird pushed back its wings, stuck out its beak and sang a song:

'Na-na, na-na-na.'

The hunter did not like the sound of the song. He wondered if the bird was making fun of him.

'Don't sing that again, or you'll be sorry,' he called up to the bird.

But the bird pushed back its wings, stuck out its beak and sang the song again.

'Na-na, na-na-na.'

'Once more,' he shouted, 'and you're dead meat!'

When the bird sang the song again the hunter aimed his bow and arrow and shot the bird straight though the heart.

The bird fell to the ground and lay there still and unmoving.

'That'll teach you,' said the hunter. He put the bird in his sack, threw the sack over his shoulder and started off for home.

As he walked he heard a muffled sound coming from inside the sack:

'Na-na, na-na-na...'

The hunter felt a little irritated and resolved to put a stop to the song as soon as he got home. Inside his kitchen he put the bird on the table and plucked it. It was cold in the hut, and the hunter noticed that the plucked bird was shivering. Then a shivering sound came from the plucked bird:

'N-na-na, n-na-na-na...'

'I wish this bird would shut up,' he fumed. 'I'll cook it, then that'll be the end of it!'

He chopped up the bird into 100 pieces (not 99, not 101, but 100) and dropped them into a pot of water that was bubbling on the fire. He was just thinking about what else to put in the stew when a bubbly sound came from the pot:

'*Na-na, na-na-na.*'

Exasperated now, he took the pot into the garden, dug a hole, poured all the bits of bird into the hole and filled it in. He was walking back to the hut when a very loud but earthy sound came up through the ground. The ground seemed to be singing the song now.

'*NA-NA, NA-NA-NA.*'

Fuming and furious he dug the bird bits up, put them in a wooden box, tied it up with string and flung it into the river that flowed past the bottom of his garden. He watched it float away, smiled, and lay down in his hammock for a well-earned rest.

A few days later some fishermen were fishing in the river downstream, throwing in their nets and pulling them out, when they saw a box floating in the water. They caught it, slowly undid the string and opened the lid.

As the lid opened, to their wonder and amazement 100 tiny birds flew out, each with a golden beak, red head, blue wings and a yellow tail.

'Wow!' they said. 'What was that?'

A few days later the hunter was hunting in the woods when he came to that same tree where he first met the bird. Perched in the top branches of the tree he saw one hundred birds, each with a golden beak, red head, blue wings and a yellow tail.

'Hmmmm,' he thought, 'Now I know what those birds are. I've heard about them but didn't know what they looked like. They must be freedom birds, because they say that however hard you try to kill one, or to keep them quiet, they just keep on coming back and singing the same song.'

So the hunter didn't try and kill any more freedom birds and from then on, at least in that forest, the hunter and the freedom birds lived happily side-by-side for ever after.

How to prepare with HMSS

We suggest that you prepare your story by using four steps: hear it, then map it, then step it, then speak it.

Hear

If you have an audio version or know someone who already tells the story, then listen to it. This is the quickest and simplest way to learn the story and fits with the way that the stories have evolved through the oral tradition, being told from one teller to another. When you listen to the story, you can pick up all sorts of ideas about voice, pacing, mood and timing. As a beginner, you may simply imitate the telling which you have heard. This is fine.

If you have an audio source then listen with your eyes closed and pay attention to the images that flow through your mind as you listen. Many storytellers remember the story through this sequence of images, so it is good to pay attention to them rather than simply concentrating on the words. Do not make notes. Just listen.

It is easier to start by listening rather than reading, but if you have only a written source then read it through a few times, again trying to be aware of the flow of images as you read. Some find it more absorbing to read it out loud. What does the story look like to you?

On pages 12 and 13 is the text for *The Freedom Song*. Listen to the version on the Story Museum website: **www.storymuseum.org.uk/1001stories** However, if you can't listen to the audio online, then read it through a few times out loud before going on to the next step.

Map

A story map gives a quick, simple picture of the key moments in the story – not everything in the tale – just the main things that need to be remembered, in sequence, for the plot to work.

Your map should take 5–10 minutes, not more. It's just a quick 'note-to-self'.

Most of your map should be a series of little icons and pictures linked together by arrows around or across the page. Where possible try to stick to images and avoid writing words if you can.

The act of creating a map does two important things. First, it reinforces your visual memory of the story by revising the images in your mind and putting them down on paper. Second, it enables you to condense and summarise the plot into a few easy-to-remember images that will help to recollect the whole story in all its detail. All that really matters is that when you look at the map, you understand it. The map is just for you.

On the opposite page there's a map one of us did for *The Freedom Song*. It is important that you draw your own map, as processing the tale and reconstructing it usually helps you to memorise the plot pattern.

The Freedom Song

Stepping The Freedom Song

1. Shoot
Hunter shoots annoying bird

2. Sack
Puts bird in the sack

3. Pluck
He plucks the bird, but it keeps singing

4. Chop
He chops it up, but it still sings

5. Bury
He buries it, but it still sings

6. Throwing
He throws it into the river

7. Wow
Fishermen open box

8. Freedom
Hunter understands the freedom bird

Step

Stepping takes you through the main story sequence again, this time using body gestures and sounds as markers of key story moments. This is a really powerful, fast and efficient way of remembering, as well as being good fun.

Choose the first important moment in the story and find a body gesture that reminds you of that moment, together with a single word or sentence.

When you have decided on your gesture and word(s) take a step forward and repeat for the second key moment. Remember, it's just the key moments. There's no unique way to do this – it's right if it works for you. Step though the story like this three or four times until you can do it easily.

You can see one of us stepping out *The Freedom Song* on the Story Museum website – **www.storymuseum.org.uk/1001stories** – as an example. (See the opposite page for a pictorial example.)

When people start stepping a story they sometimes start by speaking through the whole of the story with all the details, sort of miming the story as they go. If you like doing this then that's fine. Do that first but then try and condense the story down to a few marker moments.

Stepping gets your body involved in remembering the story, which is important for storytelling. When you tell a story, your body is involved and communicates as much with its movements as your voice does with its words. After stepping, your body will remember the story movements and naturally move that way when you tell. That movement in turn will trigger your memory of what happens. It all helps your body support your communication when you tell the story to an audience.

Notice what happens when you step. For many people it's like putting a DVD on fast-forward and stopping it every now and then. You mark your main moments and your mind fills in the gaps. Each step contains a thousand pictures and each picture a thousand words.

Speak

Now focus on speaking the story. If possible, practise telling while standing up: this gets your whole body involved which gives you more power when telling if you need it. Sitting, you have much less body to work with.

When you tell a story, at least when you are learning, always start with the past tense – 'Once there was a boy called Jack,' etc. Later, you may vary this but both you and your students need to master this simplest mode of telling first.

Remember, you are not trying to repeat all the words exactly from the source you used. You can if you like, or if this comes naturally, but you don't have to. Very simple early tales, such as *The Gingerbread Man,* may be so patterned that you fall into a rhythmic, repetitive flow. In the main though, the words will come out in your own way, with your voice and vocabulary. That's the fun of it. In this way our method is more like jazz music than classical. The basic plot is a given but then you can tell it in your own way. This is much quicker and easier than trying to remember every single word exactly, and is also more fun.

Some people like to walk and talk. Some lie on the sofa with their eyes closed and talk to the pictures in their minds. Some stand and talk to the wall. Some tell to a friend or to a dog. Some tell in the car when driving (but don't forget about the road!). You'll find out the ways that work for you. The main thing is to stay focused and tell the story a few times until you are happy with it. Then you might practise with a friend before telling it to your class.

That's it! That's the basic HMSS method.

Before you read on, why not try that for a few stories? You could use the three we mentioned on page 11. Hear them, map them, step them and speak them. After a few stories, you will find that the learning becomes much quicker and easier.

Tips for telling to your class

Special seating scheme

Have a different way of sitting to the usual classroom setup. The children could sit on the carpet, or you might rearrange the chairs in a special way so that there is a sense of being an audience. Better not to sit behind desks or tables, if possible. It shouldn't be too cramped. There should be space between students so they can relax and not be distracted by bumping into each other.

Vary the lighting

If you can control the light in your classroom, experiment with a little less light and have a bit more light in the storyteller's 'performance' place. This can change the mood and give a feeling of something special.

Group chant

You might try settling the group, if needed, using a group kinaesthetic chant. Here's one we heard from storyteller Mary Medlicott. You can chant these words with the following gestures:

'It's story time,'

(touch knees and clap in time)

'It's story time,'

(touch knees and clap in time)

'Look, listen, shhh!'

(point to eyes, ears and then finger over mouth)

Do this a few times with the class joining in, getting quieter and quieter until it's just a whisper. Also, do it with JOY. It should be heartfelt, not robotic.

Musical sounds

Another way to settle a group is to use sound from an instrument. For example, you could use a drum pulse, a simple tune on a guitar, a recorder or a Tibetan ringing bowl. This can bring a gentle magic to the room.

Remember the story is wonderful

Before you start, please remember to love and trust the story. This may sound a bit naff, but it isn't. As a storyteller, you are trying to communicate something memorable and wonderful to your audience. If you have the feeling that it is a great story and that you are happy to be sharing it with others, then your audience will feel it and be open to having a good experience.

Clarity with starting and finishing

Your first sentence should be clear, firm and confident. Practise the first few sentences word-for-word. After that most stories will pretty much tell themselves. It can also be helpful to rehearse the ending.

Eye contact

Remember to make eye contact with your audience before you start and continue this throughout the story. You can scan the whole audience in a moment, rather than staring at someone. The point is to connect with the audience and let them feel that connection. This makes storytelling precious and personal. It also helps you sense the mood, know how to respond, as well as noticing when Johnny is poking Jimmy in the ribs. Eye contact and using the whole body freely for expression are what makes storytelling so different from reading a book to a class.

Standing or sitting?

As we mentioned, many beginners feel more comfortable sitting down. You can tell sitting, if you like, but standing gives you the use of your whole body when delivering the story. This can make a story more engaging with a wider range of gestures and options for characterisation. Give it a try a few times and you may never look back!

Perfect or good enough?

If you are prone to merciless self-criticism, then please remember that you don't need to be the perfect storyteller. You are not a professional storyteller who has spent many years practising and honing a performance talent. You do not need to be that. Your job as a teacher is to give your students a good enough experience of a story to enable them to say, 'That was good, I'd like to do that too.' If they outshine their teacher then you can be really proud!

It's fine to be nervous. It's fine to make mistakes. That's all normal. As a role model, you can show them nervousness, show them mistakes and show them that you keep going anyway and don't give up. Storytelling can sometimes come from a very vulnerable place and that takes courage. Be open with your students about your nerves and it will help them to find that same courage.

After the telling

When you have finished the telling, it's good to have a regular feedback routine. This demonstrates to the class that it's OK to have feedback. It enables them to try out their positive feedback skills on you before they use them on one another. It will also help you develop as a storyteller. Watching and reflecting on the telling can help your audience develop ideas and a reflective response towards stories.

Feedback sessions also provide an immediate 'playback' moment in your audience's mind which will help them remember the story for themselves.

If you also tell the class before the telling that you will be asking particular questions afterwards, it gives an extra dimension of purposefulness to their listening. We like the following feedback routines, depending on the audience and situation:

What were your favourite moments?

You might ask for one-sentence answers to practise concision, enable more inclusion and reduce restlessness. For example, from *The Freedom Song* responses might include: 'When the birds came out of the box', 'When the hunter chopped up the bird', 'When the ground sang', etc.

What was your favourite moment and why?

This is a higher order response to the one above and requires an ability to name a reason for a preference. It could be a feeling like, 'I felt excited when the birds flew out', or it could be a preference like, 'I love blood and gore'. It could be an understanding like, 'I suddenly understood what the story meant at the end'. You can model various kinds of 'why' answers to give the idea.

What did you like about the way that the story was told?

Here you invite students to explore technique a little bit. For example, 'I liked the voice she made for the giant', 'I liked joining in with the song because it was fun', 'I liked the drum beat which made it exciting', 'I liked the description of the witch's nose because it was funny'. All this builds self-awareness and teaches pupils to reflect on how stories become great.

If you were telling the story, what would you change or add to the way it was told?

This is a way of generating new ideas. Obviously, the phrasing is there to reduce the feeling of criticising the teller. We all tell differently and that is fine. This can help the students make plans for their own telling and develop a critical vocabulary around storytelling. Again, you can model this first. For example, you might say, 'I'd use a wicked voice for the witch', 'I'd add more description of the fishermen and their nets', 'I'd pause after the birds flew away', 'I'd sing a song halfway through', 'I'd end the story with the moral', 'I wouldn't end the story with the moral', and so on.

It is good to affirm that there are no wrong questions or answers here, neither are we expressing judgement. How I tell a story is always going to be different from how you tell a story and that's fine. That's how it is.

Feedback like this helps establish a routine of positive response tasks which can engage the group and promote a playful feeling of safety and support. That's what you want to have in order to kick-start your storytelling classroom.

Types of story and how to tell them

Some people find it helpful to distinguish between three types of stories:

➤ communal chant stories

➤ participative stories

➤ independent telling

Communal stories

These are told together by the whole class more or less word-for-word, chanted a bit like a nursery rhyme, usually with particular movements to go with the words. Some teachers use them a lot and find them really helpful. Others never use them. There's no one right way in this. You might try a few and decide for yourself.

Communal stories have the advantage of quickly allowing a class to have a positive experience of telling a whole story without having the potential anxiety and challenge of telling a story alone. A restless class may also be easier to manage chanting a communal story together as everyone is telling so there is no element of silent listening involved. For these reasons, some teachers like to start with chanted stories.

You can see an example of communal chanting style for *The Little Red Hen* on the Story Museum website. There are also lots of examples of communal chanting to be found on the web. These are all simple repeating stories.

Here are a few favourites that can be told communally:

➤ *The Little Red Hen*

➤ *Gingerbread Man*

➤ *The Noisy House*

➤ *Three Little Pigs*

➤ *The Billy Goats Gruff*

➤ *The Giant Turnip*

➤ *Snip-snip*

➤ *Monkeys and Hats*

These can all be listened to on the Story Museum website: www.storymuseum.org.uk/1001stories

Of course, if you like, once you have chanted them with your class you can then move on to the stepping, mapping and independent retelling.

Communal stories do have some disadvantages. The teacher has to learn the words and gestures exactly, which takes time unless someone can show you (and then it's really quick). The ability to join in with a group does not mean full active mastery of the language pattern. However, these tales can be told as a class, in story circles and then by pairs or individuals. Encourage students to adapt the story and make it their own.

Participative stories

Many traditional tales have elements which include audience participation in various ways. This helps keep the audience engaged and involved and can be lots of fun. These ways include:

Repeating chants

For example:

'Run, run as fast as you can, you can't catch me I'm the gingerbread man.'

Little songs

For example, in the version of *The Billy Goats Gruff* on the Story Museum website, there's a song which goes like this:

'I'm going to the hill where the grass is long and green.
I'm going to the hill, it's the best we've ever seen.'

Sound effects

Ask,

'What did the wind sound like?'

or say,

'Let's hear the rooster crow!' or,
'What does the wolf sound like?'

Prediction

Ask what the audience thinks will happen next. Where this is a repeating story it is a chance for them to rehearse the repetition.

For example,

'What did the wolf say next?'

Description

Ask about a detail. For example,

'What colour do you think the little hen was?'

Additions

Invite them to add something new to the story. For example, say,

'Once there was a boy called ...' (pause), 'What shall we call him?'

Gestures

Get the audience to join in with movements. For example, if there is a bird in the story you can say, 'Now put back your wings and flap them like the bird.' In participative stories, most of the story can be improvised. However there may be particular lines to be remembered exactly for the audience to join in with.

In *The Freedom Song*, there are many ways to get the audience involved. Here are three examples:

1. Every time the bird sings, get the audience to sing the song with you. When it sings from the sack it can be a muffled song, from the table a shivery song, from the pot a bubbly song, from the ground an earthy song and back on the tree, a chirpy song.

2. When the bird pushes back its wings and pokes out its beak, you can get the audience to copy you doing that.

3. Every now and then, ask them, 'How do you think the hunter was feeling?'

Once you get used to it, getting the audience to join in becomes natural and instinctive. You will learn to do this as and when you need to, depending on the audience mood. But when you are learning, it helps to plan in advance.

Independent telling

Here the story is told to a mainly silent audience and can be told completely in the storyteller's words, improvised each time. It is always possible to add 'joining in' elements, if you feel your audience needs them to have a better experience.

Remember that it's up to you how much you improvise. Some people start off storytelling by sticking closely to the way they heard it told and only start innovating after a while. That's a good way to learn, by picking up the ways of more experienced tellers.

Some ways to refine and develop your story

There's no need to use this section unless you feel like it. You will be fine just using HMSS. However, if you want to think about the story a bit more, here are some ways to do so. They will help you teach storytelling to your class as well.

The plot matrix

The plot matrix can be used in lots of ways to understand and create stories. In this situation, it can be used as a checklist of questions to help you look at your story and think about how to make it work best. Here's the matrix:

1 Where (setting)	2 Who (character)	3 What (problem/want/need/dilemma)
4 Obstacle(s)	5 Setback(s)	6 Helper
7 Solution (resolution of main problem)	8 Ending (how do we leave the story?)	9 Learning (lessons, moral)

Or to put it another way:

Once there was person who lived in a particular place and had an important problem. There were reasons why this problem was difficult to solve. When attempts were made to solve it, setbacks were encountered, and a helper may have appeared. Finally, the problem was resolved (or not) and the story came to an end. Things were learned both by that person and by us.

These nine steps can be seen as nine friends that help make a story great. If you understand these nine elements of your story, it can help you think about how to tell it.

The three most important steps are Who (2), What (3) and Solution (7), so start with them:

Who (character)

Characters matter hugely in storytelling. Your audience has to get a feel for what a character is like and what he or she is feeling as the story progresses. They have to buy into the character and care about what happens to them.

So, think about your main characters, their main qualities, and how you will evoke them clearly in their actions and speech, and in your narration. There is no one right answer to this. In *The Freedom Song*, for example, the hunter can be an angry, impatient or foolish man. It's up to you!

You could try and give your character a voice, clearly different from the narrator, and perhaps a posture to go with it. That can really help bring the character to life.

What (problem)

The 'what' step of the matrix covers the key issue, problem, dilemma or thing around which the plot turns. It is usually something important to the character, which is wanted or not wanted. The key question is, 'Why does this matter?' or to put it another way, 'Why is it important to the character and the audience, and how can that importance be communicated in the telling?'

For example, in *The Freedom Song*, the main problem is based around an annoying sound that won't stop. It becomes important as the hunter gets more and more wound up, but in doing so only makes things worse. This feeling needs to be expressed in the telling for the story to work well. In life, we get wound up in this way, so the story echoes our own experience and we can identify with the plot.

The quality of the main character and the core problem are intimately linked. They have to work together to set up the story. Here plausibility is important. If the hunter was a relaxed, patient man, then the story wouldn't work!

Chapter 2   How to learn a story

Solution

The resolution of 'what' is probably the third most important element in the matrix. The main question here is usually, 'What is it that has changed?' Often there is some change in character or an act of learning which enables the problem to be solved. In the case of tragedy, a persistent character flaw usually prevents the resolution of the problem. In *The Freedom Song*, the hunter changes his attitude to the annoying song, reframes it and accepts it. Again, being

clear about how that solution works will help you think about how to tell it.

You can also use the whole matrix to look at how your story works. For *The Freedom Song* you could set up the matrix like the one below. This is just one personal take on the story – you would doubtless do it differently.

We will come back to the matrix later, when we explore innovation and invention.

1 Where	2 Who	3 What
Generic forest setting. Trees, animals, birds and a prey vs. predator mood.	Proud and arrogant hunter used to getting his own way and being the best. Underneath, he has an issue with teasing.	He tries to use force to stop an annoying song that he takes personally. Maybe this triggers his teasing issues.
4 Obstacle(s)	**5 Setback(s)**	**6 Helper**
The song keeps coming back.	The song seems worse for the hunter each time.	He remembers his mum's advice about freedom birds.
7 Solution	**8 Ending**	**9 Learning**
Acceptance	Harmony	You can't kill freedom – if you try, it can make things worse.

Key moments and moods

Some tellers like to think through the key moments in the story and define their moods, so they are clearer about this when they tell the story.

These can be added to a story map, or listed separately. Then you must think about what kind of things you need to describe at those moments in order to make them work. What do the characters have to say? What is the overall mood of that moment (exciting, funny, sad, sensual, happy, frightening)? How can you evoke the mood you are aiming for? Try writing the mood of each step on your map and practise putting that into your telling.

In *The Freedom Song*, a teller could aim for the moods listed in the table (right). The following page has a story map of *The Freedom Song*, with moods added.

Key moment	Mood
Hunter sees bird	Beautiful
Bird sings	Comic
Hunter shoots annoying bird	Sad, violent
Bird sings from sack	Comic
He plucks the bird, but it sings	Comic
He chops it up	Fury
It still sings	Comic
He buries it but it still sings	Mysterious
He throws it into the river	Relief
Fishermen open the box	Wonder
Hunter understands the freedom bird	Happy, wise

The Freedom Song
with moods

Chapter 3

Games and warm-ups

Storytelling 'starters'

In this chapter, we describe a set of 'warm-up' exercises that you'll need in your storytelling classroom. Please don't skip this chapter. Warm-ups get body and mind ready for storytelling and help you learn to manage storytelling in the class. They also model playfulness, spontaneity and appreciation, as well as developing the core skills of speaking and listening.

Exercises here include:

➤ 'Tell me more' (truth)

➤ 'Tell me more' (lies)

➤ Stories from everyday objects

➤ Stories from pictures

➤ Who, what, where exercises

➤ Reflecting and copying games

➤ Conversation and dialogue games

➤ Whole group re-enactment

➤ Guessing games

➤ Story making games

You need to have a repertoire of warm-up exercises to use in order to build an atmosphere of playfulness, trust and enjoyment. They will also help strengthen the core skills of storytelling and storymaking:

Speaking
Listening
Innovation
Invention

They can be used before or during a story session, and can also be used as time-filler activities at other times in the day.

If you are new to such games then you will probably want to use some of the ones we have listed. As you become familiar with the range of techniques, you will start to invent your own.

A key principle in these games is to devise activities where everyone feels engaged and derives pleasure from that engagement. This usually means that when the person is telling a story, the listeners have a purposeful task to do while listening. Devising and managing such response tasks is a key element of the storytelling classroom.

Storytelling involves the interaction of voice, body and mind. These exercises and games provide various ways to practise all three in a way that is designed to minimise anxiety and fear of failure and increase the chances of a good experience for all.

These exercises are also warm-ups for you as a teacher, enabling you to practise developing playful engagement skills in your class and building a sense of fun, safety, responsiveness and pleasure which will serve you well in all your teaching activities. We have divided them into questioning games, reflection and copying games, whole group re-enactment, guessing games and storymaking games.

Questioning games

Confident questioning and answering is a key skill for trying to understand the world we live in, whether in the classroom or outside. Any kind of investigation and exploration is driven by questions and answers in various forms. In addition, good conversation usually involves a measure of questioning and answering. It is also a key social skill.

In storytelling, a measure of questioning and answering is both used to evolve settings, characters, dilemmas and plots. As stories evolve, they naturally provoke a multitude of questions which the storyteller seeks to answer. Questions will also naturally provoke more stories.

Tell me more (truth)

This is one of our favourite games and a good one to start with. It's normally played in pairs with a storyteller and a listener or, if need be, in a group of three (storyteller, listener and helper). One great thing about this game is that it teaches the basics of conversation: once you know it, you can always find something to say. For those who struggle in social situations it can be a godsend. A parent said that 'Tell me more' enabled her to start talking again to her ten-year-old son with whom all communication had stopped.

How to play:

1. Divide into pairs and decide who is the storyteller and who is the listener.

2. The storyteller then speaks one or two sentences about themselves.

'My name is Chris and I live in Oxford in a little house near the park. My daughters' names are Natalie and Tamara.'

3. The listener then chooses a word from the two sentences which they would like to hear more about. Then they say, 'Tell me more about ...' and name the word.

'Tell me more about Oxford.'
or
'Tell me more about Tamara.'
or
'Tell me more about the park.'

4. The storyteller then gives another sentence or two about the new word.

'Oxford is a town on a big river where I like to go for a walk early in the morning.'

5. The listener then chooses another word and the storyteller gives another sentence.

In this way, a whole sequence of questions and answers might be:

Q: Tell me more about the river.

A: The river Thames goes all the way to London and once I travelled down the river for a week in a canoe.

Q: Tell me more about the canoe.

A: It was a big red canoe that a friend gave me when he left the country.

Q: Tell me more about the friend.

A: He was a German teacher at a school in Abingdon.

Q: Tell me more about Abingdon...

If the dialogue gets stuck (when someone can't think of a question or can't think of an answer) then go back to the beginning and start again.

Sometimes the stories that emerge during 'Tell me more' are fairly random sets of memory fragments. Sometimes a coherent story is produced. Either way is fine. It's all about playing about with language and not worrying too much about what happens.

This can be a good exercise to begin with because it starts with details of the storyteller's own life, so there is always something there to start talking about. As for the questioners, they just have to pick a word rather than invent a more complex question, so the whole thing is designed as a good starting game.

When the game is finished, ask the listeners to choose a favourite word that they have heard from the whole interaction and name it to the storyteller. This is important because it signals that the listener has received pleasure from the game, which is likely to reassure a nervous storyteller. Again, this task does not need a complex level of appreciation. It simply involves choosing a word.

Next, play the game again with the roles reversed.

Once everyone has had a go at being a storyteller and a listener, you might explore what the experience was like for the class. This helps them acknowledge and celebrate things which were enjoyed while giving a chance to identify and work with any difficulties. Such feedback also helps validate the students' experience as being both of importance and of interest.

Questions could include:

How did it feel?

What did you like?

What was difficult?

Sometimes it's good to use a reflecting circle to share these responses, enabling a more collective affirmation of the experience. (See more on reflecting circles on page 30). This can raise lots of energy if the class is a little flat.

There are an infinite number of ways you can vary this game by changing the instructions to the storyteller and the instructions to the listener, but it's best to start with the simplest version and keep everyone on board. High achievers can do a lot with even the simplest version above.

Examples of variations in the starting sentence:

➤ Sentence about what you did last week
➤ Sentence about something happy that you remember
➤ Sentence about a time of difficulty
➤ Sentence about what you'd like to do at playtime
➤ Sentence about your favourite toy
➤ Sentence about your mum

You can also vary the telling instruction:

➤ One sentence
➤ A few sentences
➤ Talk for ten seconds
➤ Talk until you are interrupted

Options for the listener include:

➤ Choose a favourite word
➤ Choose a word you want to know more about
➤ Choose a word that will help tell a good story

Calibrating for age and ability

It is usually good to demonstrate the game before asking pairs to play it. This gives students who might struggle to make things up a chance to copy what you say. In terms of the three 'I's model (imitation, innovation, invention) this gives students an opportunity to imitate first before starting to innovate.

For example for a four- or five-year-old you might demonstrate like this:

'My name is Chris and I live in a house with a green door, windows and a garden. I live with my two daughters, a cat and some goldfish.'

Q: Tell me more about the house.

A: Inside my house there is a kitchen, a TV room, a bathroom and three bedrooms.

Q: Tell me more about the kitchen.

A: In the kitchen there is a fridge, a cooker, a sink and a table.

Q: Tell me more about the fridge.

A: In the fridge there is milk, butter, etc.

In this way you can model something that a young child can more or less copy to get started.

Tell me more (lies)

TMM Lies is basically the same as TMM Truth, except that the storyteller makes up a character idea and talks about that:

'My name is Gladys and I am a world champion disco dancer.'

'My name is Thor and I am a fighter with a big hammer.'

Otherwise, the game is played in the same way. You can help encourage your class to be daring, playful and imaginative if you do the same in your demo. It's important that they get the idea

that they are free to play in pretty much any way they like and it will be OK.

If there is a danger of uncomfortable teasing you might have a ground rule that they must never use the name of someone in the room.

Some students love TMM Truth and some prefer TMM Lies. It's good to play both regularly to cater for both tastes. The more the listeners soak up ideas in this game the more they will have to say next time.

Stories from everyday objects

This is a great game to develop 'inventions'. Initially, work with the whole class. Here's a suggestion:

Choose a shoe from a volunteer and put it in front of the class or in the centre of the circle.

Start with something like:

'This shoe is now a story shoe and we're going to find out what story it comes from. I will ask questions and I want you to put your hand up if you have an idea for an answer. I'll take a few suggestions then choose one and ask another question.'

Now as the leader you have to sort out your questions so they help to make a story. Remember the plot matrix: this is a good thing to have in mind. Here's a reminder:

1 Where	2 Who	3 What
4 Obstacle(s)	5 Setback(s)	6 Helper
7 Solution	8 Ending	9 Learning

You need a beginning (character, setting, problem) a middle (obstacles, setbacks and helpers), and an end (resolution, ending and learning).

So start by establishing character and place, asking questions like:

➤ Who does the shoe belong to?

➤ What's their name?

➤ Where do they live?

➤ Who do they live with?

➤ What do they like?

➤ What do they hate?

Then move on to the problem. You might ask:

X has something really important to them that they really want or really don't want. What is it?

Why is it important?

X tries a way of solving the problem but it proves difficult. What does X try and what happens?

What happens next?

Then move on to the solution, with questions like:

Does someone come to help?

Who and how?

How is the problem finally resolved (or not)?

What was learned?

What's great about this game is the enthusiasm and excitement generated in the whole class with urgent pleas for inclusion of various ideas. Obviously you can use any object to start with in future games.

If you hand over questioning to a student, you might explain the matrix principle so they establish a beginning, middle and end or maybe have the matrix on the wall to remind them.

You could also list questions for each category for those who get stuck, and put them up on the wall too.

Once the class gets really good at this, split them into small groups of, say, five to seven and have them play the game separately and then come back and tell the class their story.

Establish the ground rule that the questioner is in charge of the decision on which answer to take.

It's really good to model choosing from a number of answers: this is the creative process we all need to learn, generating a number of ideas and then choosing the best, not just accepting any old idea. This needs confidence and the capacity of those whose idea is not chosen, to accept it. It's good to emphasise that everyone is different and just because an idea is not chosen, it doesn't mean that it isn't any good.

Stories from pictures

You can use a photo, a piece of art or a picture created in the class. Choose the right picture for your class. Whatever the picture is, the process is similar to that above with the everyday object, except that with the picture there are more options. It can be a place, a house, a character or a moment in a story with all sorts of things going on. You can ask lots of questions about what things can be seen in the picture.

This can be great for young children for whom it may be a big achievement to name elements of the picture successfully. You can then spend more time on what happens next and on mature plot questions.

You can also use a story map and do the same thing. There are plenty on the Story Museum website:
www.storymuseum.org.uk/1001stories

Who, what, where, when

Another way of practising storymaking is to define the types of questions that can be asked. So for example, 'Tell me more' can be played with the questioner only able to ask questions starting with who, what, where, or when. This can be more challenging to the storyteller than the original game so you have to model this carefully and make sure storytellers don't get too stuck and start to panic. You can always allow an 'I don't know,' answer if the teller can't think of a question.

You can also play it in groups of three or four with listeners making suggestions for the storyteller to choose from if they get stuck. This can build a good supportive teamwork feeling in the group, so long as levels of anxiety and fear of ridicule are manageable.

Reflection and copying games

These games allow a great deal of imitation, a good place to start with storytelling. Copying can be collective or individual, and can involve sound, word, sentence, tune, gesture and movement in any combination and these are the basics that the storyteller uses.

Copying provides a clear and playful response task for listeners and enables fragments of language and gesture to be actively learned.

Collective reflection provides a kind of group safety which is helpful for those who might initially feel anxious and exposed by individual reflection.

The reflecting circle

The basic principle here involves the class standing in a circle. Initially the teacher will do something and everyone else then copies it, either moving with the teacher or echoing it back. It's a good way to strengthen confident physicality.

Here's one way to get a reflecting circle started:

1. Ask the class to stand in a circle

2. Say:

'I want you all to be my mirror – move silently as I move.'

3. Silently move your body in all sorts of ways – stretching, miming, clowning around. Stay more or less on the spot so the circle stays intact. This gives the group a feeling that this will be fun. If you like, hand over the leadership to a student and let them lead the class for a bit. Notice any reluctant movers and see if you can find movements where they feel comfortable.

4. Next teach them the echo principle. Say:

'Now I am going to make a movement. The first time, watch me do it. The second time, move with me.'

Think of a simple gesture like drinking from a cup and have them echo it with you. Repeat for various everyday movements.

5. Now continue but add a sound for them to copy. For example:

➤ drink a cup of tea and make a slurping noise
➤ run on the spot with loud puffing
➤ shoot and make a bang

6. When this is going well, continue with words and then with sentences. You can choose lines and movements from a well known story. For example, from *Little Red Riding Hood*:

Wagging finger –

You will go to your grandma!

Showing teeth and claws –

Where are you going little girl?

Puzzled and shaking –

What big ears you have!

Pouncing –

All the better to eat you with!

By now we are mixing body and voice to tell fragments of a story, finding the feeling and voice of the character and a movement to go with it. These are the basics of storytelling, bringing together body, voice and imagination.

You can also use the reflecting circle to check-in on how the group is feeling or what they are thinking.

For example:

How are you feeling? I am feeling ...

(add word and gesture)

What was that experience like? It was ...

(add word and gesture)

Tell us something that happened since we met last ...

(add sentence and gestures)

Tell us something good and something bad that has happened to you with a word for each ...

(add two words and gestures)

After storytelling of any kind we can also pool responses in the circle in the same way, using prompts like:

What was your favourite word?

(reflect with gesture)

What was your favourite moment?

(sentence and gesture)

Who was you favourite character?

(name and gesture)

What did you like about the way the tale was told?

(phrase and gesture)

Passing around the circle

Passing sounds, movements or words around a circle can be a way of initiating non-simultaneous responses. However, a circle of 30 takes a long time to go round and your class may find the waiting difficult.

Reflecting in small groups

You can use the same principles of reflecting when working in pairs or small groups. One student initiates and the other copies with a variety of sequences. This needs quite a lot of concentration in a classroom as groups can easily distract each other, especially if noise is involved. But the great thing about small group reflecting is that the groups can work out a sequence of noises or movements and then share them back with the larger circle. This can give a sense of purpose and excitement to the small group work and provide more opportunities for individual initiative.

Examples might include working out a reflecting mime in a small group that tells a known story (maximum 1 minute) and then have it reflected back by the whole class.

Yes, let's!

'Yes, let's'! is an energising warm-up which can allow students to explore unconditional playfulness. In 'Yes, let's', we divide up into pairs and each pair thinks of something that they'd like everyone to do. Then one pair shouts out their wish. For example:

'Let's all jump up and down and pretend that we are rabbits!'

Then everyone calls out

'Yes, let's'!

with huge enthusiasm and pretends to be rabbits.

Then another group might call out,

'Let's all flap our wings and make a bird noise,'

and everyone replies,

'Yes, let's!'

And so on ...

This can raise a lot of joy and can be helpful if the class is sleepy.

Conversation and dialogue games

Getting characters to speak convincingly and with clarity of feeling is key to good storytelling. You want to play speech and dialogue games of various kinds to get the students used to making up speech. Through their playing, they will themselves internalise new ideas for their own speech and storytelling. We can usually do this quite naturally.

Cocktail party

This is quite quick and relaxed and can be a good way to start.

1. Let everyone choose a character, allocate known characters (fairytale characters work well or ones from class books), or play 'Tell me more (lies)' (page 28) to create a character.

2. Then ask your class to imagine they are walking around the room at a party where they don't know anyone. How will their character walk? Show them a few options (slow, fast, relaxed, stiff, happy, sad and so on).

3. Then say something like:

'Now I am going to play the drum,' (so yes, you need a drum or some instrument!) 'and I want you to walk around as your character would until the drum stops, then turn to somebody near you and talk to them as your character.'

4. You can role-play some demonstration conversations to give ideas and then let the class have a go.

5. After a few seconds of conversation, say:

'Now thank the person you met and tell them what you liked most about meeting them. When the drum plays, go back to silent walking as your character.'

6. Repeat this with various instructions.

For example:

➤ talk about what you like;

➤ talk about what you hate;

➤ talk about what you hope for;

➤ talk about where you live.

Through the conversation, they build up a picture of the character.

Finally, you might gather in a reflecting circle. Each person might give one sentence and one movement about their character to be reflected.

Role-play dialogue

Think up a situation where your class will have speech experience to draw on, for example, a mother trying to get a child to tidy their room.

Demonstrate a made-up role-play to the class with an able pupil. Repeat it a few times, then get groups to practise in pairs and perform back selected improvisations to the whole group.

Remember to try and give your audience a response task to keep their listening purposeful. For example:

➤ choose your favourite word

➤ choose your favourite moment

➤ choose your favourite gesture

➤ find the most interesting question

You can of course repeat this for known stories. Little Red Riding Hood might argue with her mum about going to see her granny. The same principles apply.

Whole group re-enactment

It is surprisingly easy to get a whole class to enact a story spontaneously without any planning and preparation at all – the main thing is that the storyteller/teacher feels comfortable with the way of working.

You can do it like this:

1. Sit in a circle

2. Say,

'Now I am going to tell the story of Little Red Riding Hood. Every time I need a character or object in the story I will ask someone to get up and play that role. The stage is the middle of the circle. When I need something, I'll stop the story and look for volunteers.'

3. Now start the story:

'Once upon a time Little Red Riding Hood's mother was making a cake in the kitchen,'

(pause and wait for a volunteer, who will get into the circle and mime mixing a cake).

'Little Red Riding Hood was playing in the garden,'

(get a volunteer to play in the circle while the mum mixes).

'Then Mum asked Little Red Riding Hood to come inside,'

(pause – let the actor say the line).

'Inside they had a chat about her granny,'

(let them improvise a conversation if they are able, or else tell them what to say).

And so on...

This makes excellent theatre, as there is a tension of unpredictability and live improvisation which is usually exciting. If speech is too difficult then you can do it just with mime first.

All this is great for sequencing skills, learning a story, improvising elements and physically internalising the story.

Guessing games

Guessing games can be a good way of generating group interest, as a story element is explored by a group member. Almost anything can be a subject of guessing.

Here are some examples:

Guess the emotion

Name a list of, say, ten emotions and then get someone to stand up and evoke one of those feelings silently. Give the audience three guesses. Make it clear that it is not a competition to guess correctly. It's just a way of learning about how to communicate feelings.

Guess the character

The same principle, but now choose a character from a story or stories that all the class members know. Mime or enact a moment with that character and give three guesses for recognising the character and moment in the story.

Guess the lie

Say three sentences – two of them are true and one is a lie. The pupils must guess the lie (this can be done in pairs if it works better).

Guessing adds a touch of drama and uncertainty which can be fun to play with.

Storymaking games

Fortunately/unfortunately

This is a great game for getting free imagination going. Play with an odd number of people, perhaps 5 or 7. Introduce a character and then take turns to describe alternately fortunate and unfortunate things to happen to the character, without killing them.

For example:

Once there was a boy called Jack.

Unfortunately, one day he fell down a hole.

Fortunately, at the bottom of the hole was a diamond.

Unfortunately, it was sharp and he cut his finger on it.

Fortunately, his mum found him bleeding and took him to the hospital.

Unfortunately, the police saw the diamond and put him in jail.

Fortunately, the bars on his window were broken and he escaped.

And so on ...

Demonstrate to the class, play in small groups and then have a story summary fed back to the whole class.

This can also be played in pairs, physically miming the story as they invent it. This needs lots of space to prevent collisions, but is loads of fun and great for energetic students who love physical activity.

Show and tell with a twist

Ask pupils to tell news or bring in an object from home to talk about. The twist is to add a little fantasy into the story.

First tell them a true story about yourself or about an object you have brought, but add some fantasy elements: a pink, talking rabbit appearing on the doorstep, a tiny dinosaur turning up in the supermarket, and so on.

After your telling, ask your pupils to reflect upon their favourite bit of the story, which bits were true and which were made up, how the story could have been improved, and so on. Then, let them have a go.

If you use an object, you might model telling a story of how you came by it with a few made-up elements. If you want to structure it, you might tell of some fantastic discovery you have made about it, what the object does and something amazing that has happened to you while using it.

After your little story, let the students work out what was true and what you made up. Ask them:

'Did it sound believable when I was telling it?'

Then let the pupils have a go.

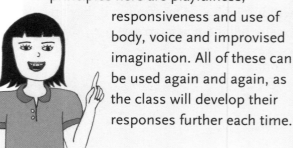

That's probably enough to begin with: get to know these, add your own favourites and then start making up your own new ones. The basic principles here are playfulness, responsiveness and use of body, voice and improvised imagination. All of these can be used again and again, as the class will develop their responses further each time.

Chapter 3   Games and warm-ups

Chapter 4

How to teach a story to your class

Hear, Map, Step, Speak

In this chapter, we explain how to get your students telling stories themselves using the Hear, Map, Step, Speak method described in Chapter 2. This mixes visual, physical and auditory modes and is a robust, fast and inclusive way of learning to retell narratives of many kinds. Once your class has learned HMSS, you will be able to use it across the curriculum for any sequence you would like the class to learn.

Method and key principles

When you teach a story to your class you can use this basic method:

1. **HEAR**: you tell the story to the class.

2. **MAP**: each student draws his or her own story map.

3. **STEP**: each student steps through the story.

4. **SPEAK**: each student tells the story a few times, independently, to a partner or group.

Remember several key principles when teaching HMSS:

➤ Be playful – the method is fun and works because it is enjoyable.

➤ Be appreciative – for most people the key obstacle to storytelling is fear of ridicule. You need to build an atmosphere of active appreciation in your classroom, modelled first by you and then taught to the class. Leave the suggestions and critical appreciation for later. In general, make feedback comments specific:

'I liked that particular word', 'I enjoyed that moment because...' and so on. 'That is good' is not enough, as it leaves the child not knowing what was good. So – be specific.

➤ Listening skills – whilst speaking the story in pairs, students need to have appropriate listening skills, including maintained eye contact, appreciative body language, and concentration on the story while it is being told. If this is difficult then it may be worth spending more time on listening games such as 'Tell me more' (p.26) to develop this skill.

➤ Modelling – always demonstrate something before you ask the class to do it. This allows those who need to, to imitate you. Innovation comes naturally once imitation is mastered.

➤ Response tasks – whenever you give your class a listening task, think about building in one or more response tasks, so that students have a purpose to their listening. The tasks need to be calibrated to your particular class's needs. Some listeners will need to be active with something to do every minute or so, others will be happy to listen for ten minutes and give feedback at the end. But always try and give listeners a specific task to think about before you start.

Your main objective when creating a storytelling classroom is to make it safe and enjoyable so that students want to tell their stories. Build a base of appreciation, security and mutual support and your class will flourish. If these basics are not in place, then take some time to build them.

Here are the four HMSS steps in more detail:

1. Hear

In step one, the students hear somebody, probably the teacher, telling the story. A person is much better than an audio or video clip. The physical presence of a storyteller creates a deeper and more intense experience, which the student can imitate if need be. Storytelling is wonderful because it involves human co-presence. Anything less is second best. The basic method for telling the story is covered in Chapter 2. Remember to explain to the class that they will be learning to tell the story. This provides a purpose for their listening. Once you have told the story and completed your feedback routine, then move on to step two.

2. Map

In step two, every student draws a map of the story. This revisits the visual memory, helping them to remember the story in terms of images rather than words. It is much more efficient than trying to memorise every single word. The pictures evoke the words quite naturally.

Shared mapping

While the class is learning this technique, it is usually a good idea to create a map (or at least part of a map) with the students, before sending them off to work on their own. This gives them ideas for how to map and also allows them to imitate your ideas if need be. In your maps use a quick, stick-figure style so that it is clear that this is not an art competition. With much younger students, draw the whole map.

1. Let's assume you have just told them *The Freedom Song*. You might then say:

   'Now we're going to draw a story map to help us remember the main things that happened. We don't need to include everything, just the key points that we need to remember. So what's the first thing that happened?'

2. Students will start with the first sentence ('Once there was a hunter,') followed by the next and the next. Keep prompting them for what happens next until you get to a key moment, for example the moment when the hunter shoots the bird.

3. Highlight that this is a key moment and draw it quickly. It should take no more than about five seconds. Emphasise that this is a key moment in the story and that when you look at it, it helps you remember all the other things that happened previously.

4. Say:

   'Now what's the next key moment?'

   Take suggestions until you get to the bird in the bag. This can be as simple as just a picture of a bag – that's enough to remember the sequence. Go on in the same way: plucking, shivering, chopping, burying and so on with quick, simple pictures.

5. Link each picture with an arrow. It may be a circle, a spiral, a zigzag or a snake – that's up to you – but the sequence must be clear. Try not to use words. We are practising using the visualising side of the brain.

Imitate or innovate?

Whether you draw the whole map or just one or two pictures is up to you. If the class is new to such mapping, you might draw half a map and then ask the students to do their own map, leaving your half for them to copy before filling the rest themselves. Sometimes, for Foundation or Year 1, you might do the whole map and let them copy it in its entirety.

Once you think the class is up to it, you can do the whole map, show the class, then put it away and ask the students to do theirs in their own way. Finally, once the class has got the hang of it, they can go straight to their own maps without any demonstrations at all, unless you have some new element you want to introduce.

For Foundation Stage and KS1 the images have to be simple enough for the students to copy and then to recognise when they look at the map. One way to make mapping easier is to draw a series of numbered circles on a page linked by arrows, each with the simple image inside it.

Here's a map inspired by Eric Carle's *The Very Hungry Caterpillar* that Foundation Stage students would be able to copy. The food sequence in the pictures is apple, pear, plum and grapes. This can be drawn on to a flipchart and then each student can copy the images into the circles on their own sheet.

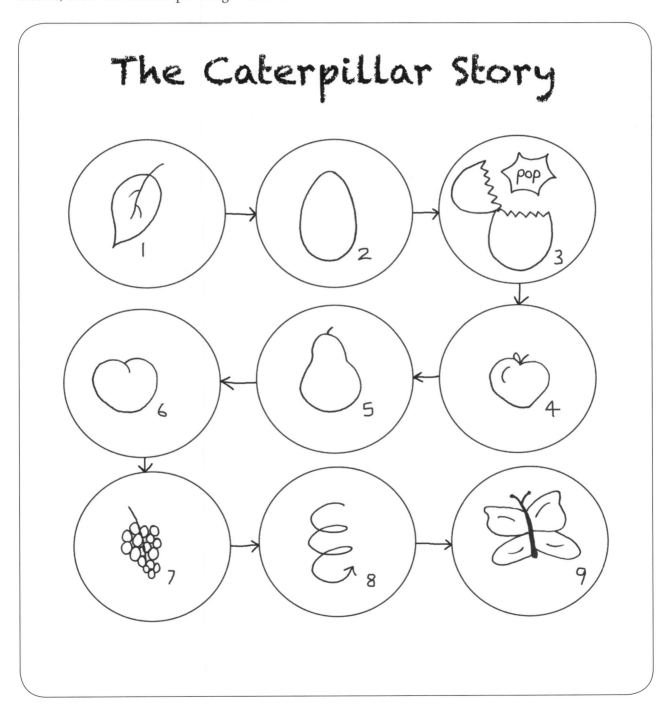

Independent mapping

Once the shared element of mapping is complete, you can ask students to create maps of their own. It's helpful to give a time limit of about five minutes so that students don't linger too much on unnecessary detail. When they have finished, ask them to explain their maps to a partner. This is to make sure they can read their own maps and to remind them of the story sequence. The response task of the listener is to ask questions if they don't understand anything and alert the mapper if a main step is missed. It's fine to edit the map during the retelling. This also helps the listener remember the sequence.

3. Step

Please don't skip this step! Story stepping is great. Students love it. It allows them to channel their physicality and creativity in an independent and playful way, which accesses deep memory elements of the mind.

During the mapping stage we reinforce the visual sequence of a story in the mind. Now we make the most of body posture and sound. We use these modes to condense the complexity of a whole story into a sequence of gestures and words. This condensing is a basic skill for study and learning.

Imitate or innovate the steps?

When you start to teach stepping, it is important that you demonstrate it yourself. Try to evoke playfulness and make it fun. You want your class to think 'That looks like fun. I'll have a go at that!' Practise various combinations of words, sounds and movements until you have something you like.

With Foundation and Year 1 students you may like initially to teach them to step a story by having them copy you exactly. This will be fun for them and naturally they will start to innovate once they have learned your version.

In Year 2 and above, many students will like to innovate from the start, making up some of their own steps, but it's still helpful to do a full stepping demonstration so that the more cautious students can start by imitating you.

If you are stepping *The Freedom Song*, try these gestures:

1. Shoot 2. Sack 3. Pluck 4. Chop

5. Bury 6. Throwing 7. Wow 8. Freedom

For the Caterpillar Story it could be:

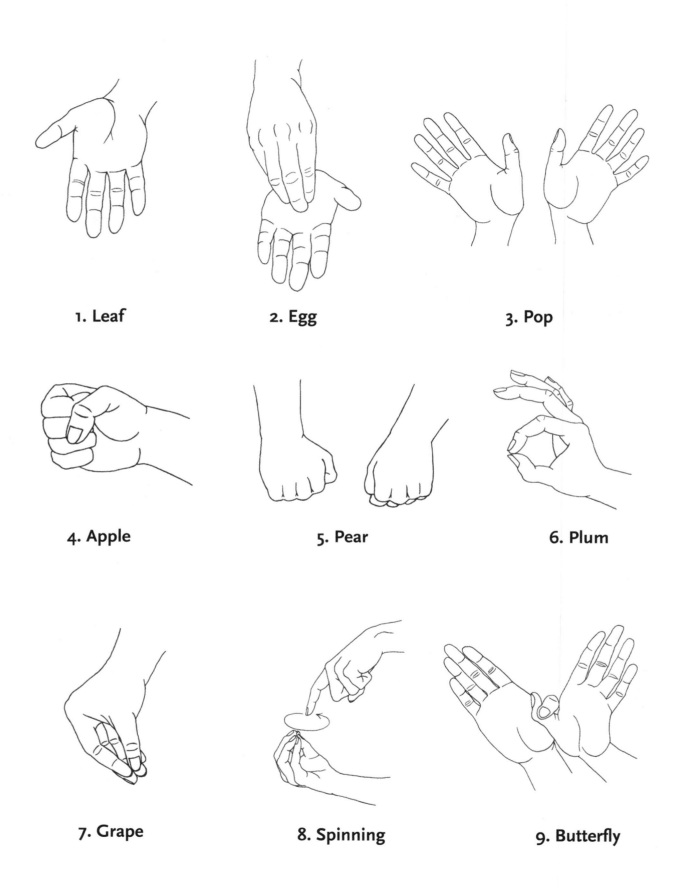

1. Leaf

2. Egg

3. Pop

4. Apple

5. Pear

6. Plum

7. Grape

8. Spinning

9. Butterfly

How to teach stepping

You need enough space for the stepping. Some primary classrooms are big enough (for 15 pairs, 10 steps each) but others get a bit cramped. Some teachers go out into the playground, some use the school hall, some use the corridors and some use two classrooms. This is the technique for teaching how to step:

1. Say:

'Imagine that there is a river in front of me. There are ten stepping stones across the river. We are now going to walk across the stones one by one.'
(Physically do this.)

2. Say:

'Each stepping stone is a key moment in the story. It might be the same moment as in your map, and it might not. What is important is that you choose the main things you need to remember, and then think of a movement and a word to go with each. Let me show you one way of doing this for The Freedom Song.'
(Demonstrate stepping the story.)

3. Say:

'Now find a partner and have a go yourself. You can do it your own way, or copy me if you like. Remember to try and end up with about ten freeze frames. Use you map to help if you like, but then put it away and step from memory.'

Give your class time to step and re-step a few times but not for long enough to lose interest.

Tips

Stepping may feel noisy and a bit chaotic at first but try to accept that. It is better for the students to experience it as a moment of freedom rather than an over-controlled task. Let them play with the idea in their own way and try not to tell them how to do it.

However clear your instructions are, many students will not step in the way you imagined. This is OK. Indeed, it is good, because many people like to do their own interpretation. Let your students develop their own ideas, so long as they are stepping and moving through the story.

Some pairs will initially do a kind of talk and walk through the story, retelling the whole thing  by recalling the words or stepping through every main image. This is fine and can be a good place to start. Once they have completed this stage then you might say: 'That's great! Now try choosing about ten key moments from the story and give each a word and a movement. Try stepping with just those ten moments.'

When someone misses something out, there's no need to mention it. Everyone can have a slightly different sequence. It doesn't really matter much if the story changes slightly. This can demonstrate innovation. Don't worry about missed bits, unless the plot collapses completely. If this happens, make a few gentle suggestions or have students revisit their map.

Giving praise for every new idea that emerges is good, especially for the first few stories. This will help those who feel nervous and exposed. Try to be specific in your praise so that it can be fully received.

Some students step faster than others. You can ask pairs who finish early to repeat a few times with improvements and then to step in more challenging ways, for example silently, or with sound effects only, or with hand gestures only.

Stepping theatre

When all the pairs have successfully completed at least one stepping of the story you can bring the class back together. Try to create a theatre-type space in your class for this stage, perhaps with students in the audience sitting in rows, or in a horseshoe. This is less intimidating than an audience behind desks. Then you can:

1. Say:

'Now we're going to watch some pairs show us their way of stepping. Afterwards, I want you to choose a favourite moment from the stepping and let us know what it is.'

2. Next, ask individual pairs to show the class their steps. Please don't interrupt or allow interruption from the audience until the pair has finished. If the pair gets stuck during the performance then join them and step with them, suggesting possible steps and movements. Afterwards take time for some audience appreciation. You can let steppers choose the people they want appreciation from, building a greater sense of autonomy.

3. Remember, every time a pair steps to the class, the whole group is remembering the sequence of the story and collecting ideas for words, sounds and gestures that they might use, so it's good to watch a few versions of stepping – you'll see how they improve with time.

4. When you have finished the stepping demos, ask for feedback to check for any obstacles and difficulties in the group. Make sure you pair up struggling steppers with confident steppers next time so that they get the idea.

Most classes love stepping. It can be used as a memory device for any kind of sequence that you want your class to learn.

Stepping variants

There is no limit to ways of stepping; you can vary your instructions to the class as they become more fluent.

Here are a few:

➤ Step with sound effects only, no words

➤ Step in silence

➤ Step with a sung line at each step

➤ Develop a dance routine by having a repeating rhythmic phrase and movement at each step

➤ Character stepping – have a character speak a line at each step

➤ Haiku stepping – compose or recite a mini poem at each step

➤ Mood stepping – name a feeling and associated movement at each step

➤ Hand gestures only

➤ Puppet stepping

Try a few of these and then make up your own!

4. Speak

After stepping comes speaking: saying the narrative out loud. The memories of listening, mapping and stepping form the basis for this stage. By now students have a clear idea of the sequence of events in the story and can draw on that when they tell. That is to say, they are able to start preparing their words and put flesh back onto the bare bones of the story. Telling in pairs or small groups is the simplest way to do this. Adults may prefer to practise alone but many primary age students struggle to retain concentration without an audience. A shared telling can be a good way to start before moving on to an independent telling. There is less risk of getting stuck or lost with the story at the beginning.

Shared paired storytelling

Demonstrate this with a volunteer before asking the class to work in pairs. The idea is similar to that of a story circle but with two people. Someone starts the story and then passes it on after a few sentences. This means that if a teller doesn't know what to say he or she just passes the story back to their partner to continue.

Start by showing the technique with a storytelling object (a stone, bowl, or pen, anything will do). Find a volunteer and start telling the story. After a couple of sentences pass the object to the volunteer and let them continue for a bit before they pass the object back to you. Once everyone has the idea, divide the class up into pairs and get them to retell the story like that. At the end of the telling, share favourite moments with the whole group.

Independent paired storytelling

Now, maybe with a new pairing, ask each student to tell the whole story. The job of the listener is to pay full attention, offer help if asked and offer feedback on their favourite moments, at the end of the telling.

Avoiding anxiety

If the pairs are struggling to focus or remember, let them tell initially from a story map before putting it away.

If anxiety levels are too high and people are freezing or reacting negatively, then go back to whole group activities for a while until group trust levels are higher. These could include:

➤ Shared telling to the whole class

➤ Group story chanting

➤ Reflecting circle – fragments of the story

➤ Whole class re-enactments

➤ Telling individual fragments of the story to the whole class

If the story is too complex then try a simpler, more physical one to start off with and chant it communally for a few days before trying shared and independent telling.

Thinking like a storyteller

The Storytelling School is all about learning to think like a storyteller, which means asking the question, 'How can I make the story better for my audience?'

By keeping this is mind, and getting the feedback after each telling, stories gradually evolve and improve, first orally and then in written form.

Giving feedback after storytelling

Constructive feedback skills are important for both the storyteller and the listener in a number of ways:

➤ Knowing that a story was listened to and enjoyed builds confidence and enjoyment of telling, reducing anxiety

➤ When an audience knows that it will be given a feedback task after a telling it encourages more purposeful listening and enables more to be learned from the listening experience

➤ Specific feedback can give ideas for ways to improve a story to achieve a particular effect

➤ Giving specific feedback helps develop ways of thinking about storytelling and a vocabulary for discussing them

➤ Being able to happily receive suggestions for ways to improve a story builds the skills of learning to consider the suggestions of others and deal with any emotional responses to perceived criticism. It also teaches the value of input from others

➤ Learning to give suggestions in a helpful way builds the skills of sharing ideas in a considerate way

➤ Learning to think like a storyteller means asking the question 'how can the story be even better?' for a given audience. Finding out about the audience's experience is a good way to learn this.

Here are some suggestions about ways to organise your feedback both from you as a teacher and from your class to one another. As a teacher you can:

➤ model a particular kind of feedback for your class to learn from

➤ give particular instructions for what kind of feedback an audience is to give after listening (whether whole class or small groups)

It's often good to give instructions to your class before the telling to give purposefulness to their listening.

Here are some options for feedback tasks:

Three foci: story, storyteller and storytelling!

In Doug Lipman's wonderful and thoughtful book, *The Storytelling Coach*, he sets out three ways of giving feedback after listening to a story:

➤ About a moment in the storytelling

➤ About the story

➤ About the storyteller

Also he suggests always starting by focusing on things you enjoy as an audience, helping with confidence and self-awareness of the storyteller's strengths.

About a storytelling moment

This is about a favourite moment in the storytelling ('I liked the way you roared/spoke/paused when Little Red Riding Hood met the wolf: it was really scary'). These tell the storyteller about how a particular bit of telling was experienced, and what worked well.

About the storyteller

However, there are not always great moments like this and you can also feedback in two other ways. You can offer general feedback on the storyteller's qualities ('I liked the way you spoke really clearly so I could easily understand your words'; 'I liked the way all the descriptions were really vivid so I could imagine them'; 'I liked the way you made eye contact with us from time to time'; 'I liked the way your gestures supported the story'). This helps the storyteller understand their own style and its strengths.

About the story

Finally, if you can't find a truthful thing to say about the first two then there is *always* something good to say about the story itself. ('I like the bit in the story where she goes into the cottage but doesn't know it's the wolf in the bed.')

So whenever a story is told in the class you can always feedback in one or more of these ways.

Once a telling has been adequately appreciated, you may want to offer suggestions. Lipman has a lovely way of doing this. He uses the word **more**,

As in, 'it would be great to have a bit more ....'

I like this way because it implies that there is something there already that is really good – in fact it is so good that you think the story needs even more of it. In this way the suggestion is more likely to be received happily and less likely to trigger self-doubt and resistance. A comment might be like this:

'I'd really like to know a bit more about the Red Riding Hood's character so I can imagine what she's like; I'd like a bit more description of what she saw in the cottage so I can imagine how she felt; I'd like to know more about how the wolf was feeling to build excitement in the story.'

If you can it's good to explain why you want more of something with language like this :

➤ because it would build tension

➤ because it would develop character

➤ because it would make it more interesting

➤ because it would help me picture it

Here's a sample checklist of aspects of performance that you or your class might feedback on. Basically a storyteller has two things to retell story with: voice and body. The challenge is to use them together to provide satisfying engagement.

They are mainly used to evoke:

➤ Action (what happened?)

➤ Description (details of sense impressions)

➤ Character (thinking, feeling, choosing, doing)

This is done with the voice of the narrator and the voices of the characters.

Here are some ways to think about the content of the feedback, to help frame your and your class's responses:

11 Aspects of storytelling performance

Here are eleven things that a storyteller learns over the years. Some of them may make a good checklist for you and your class to think about when planning, practising and thinking about storytelling.

1. Words (clear, suitable?)

2. Action (clear?)

3. Thinking and feeling of characters (clear, suitable?)

4. Narrator and character voices (clear, suitable?)

5. Descriptions (clear, suitable?)

6. Gesture and posture (clearly and suitably linked to story?)

7. Pace (varied to evoke mood and interest?)

8. Volume (varied to evoke mood and interest?)

9. Pauses (suitable?)

10. Songs/poems/music/story runs (suitable for mood and story pause?)

11. Audience engagement (suitable use of eye contact, enthusiasm and joining in strategies?)

Story matrix

You can use the story matrix to think about the story as it was told, what elements of the plot were evoked suitably and where this might be improved. Here's a sample checklist of questions:

➤ Setting – was it clear, consistent and suitable?

➤ Character – was it clear, consistent and suitable?

➤ Problem – was it and its importance clear?

➤ Obstacle – were the difficulties in solving clear enough?

➤ Helper – was the character and help given clear and suitable?

➤ Solution – was it interesting, believable, satisfying?

➤ Ending – are the resolutions and non-resolutions clear and satisfying?

➤ Learning – is it clear what qualities characters learned?

Then there is the broader question – does the whole thing fit together in a consistent and believable way?

As your class develops it's probably good for them to see professional storytellers performing live if possible or on video, so they can see how great storytelling works and begin to unpick the eleven aspects of performance and the nine steps in the matrix in practice.

But the first thing is to get going and make sure everyone is confident that they can tell a story. A good time to watch professionals is once the school has got started with their telling, then they will take lots of ideas from the teller and blend it into their own storytelling. It's good to use storytellers who are recommended by a trusted source. In England you can't do better than the Crick Crack Club storytellers for top-level performance technique (www.crickcrackclub.com).

Remember – this first stage is all about getting started, not doing perfect storytelling. Simply getting the words out with the main events is enough to start with. More is a bonus. Once everyone in your class can do that they are ready to go on to deepening.

Chapter 5

Deepening

Growing new stories

In this chapter we explain how to 'deepen' the story so that it grows in the imagination of the students and develops into a new improvised story. Over 20 different deepening exercises are described in our examples. We also show how to introduce some basic plot and character patterns, which will help with invention of new stories.

Deepening exercises

Once a story has been learned with Hear Map Step Speak or a similar approach, the students are ready to deepen their connection with it. These exercises offer various methods of exploring and retelling the story so that it grows and develops for each student in their own way, while retaining a sense of interest and variety.

In terms of language development, the deepening process allows the student to express the language patterns in the story many times so that they become securely embedded and mastered. It also helps to create a vivid and exciting connection with the story, enabling students' own retellings to improve as they put new flesh on its bones.

We have not focused on writing exercises in this section, because we generally recommend working on deepening before moving on to writing. However, that choice does depend on the class and the learning priorities. Most of these exercises can be used as a basis for a linked writing exercise if that is needed and they all support the development of language that can later be used in writing.

A repertoire of about 20 or so deepening exercises is ideal, so that you can offer your class enough variety to avoid a sense of routine repetition. We will use *The Freedom Song* story as our example, for the sake of continuity:

Character dialogue

Choose a moment in the story where two characters might speak to each other. Demonstrate with a volunteer how to make up speech on the spot, and then get students to practise in pairs before re-playing to the class, for appreciative feedback. Students might name those words or ideas that they could include in their story.

Appropriate moments could include:

➤ two fishermen discussing whether to open the box

➤ the hunter meeting a friend after burying the bird and discussing what to do

➤ the hunter telling the story to his mother

Your demonstration is important as it allows students to get ideas for their own improvisation. Choose more able students to demonstrate first so that others can copy their ideas. If you don't find improvising easy, do a bit of practice on your own and with a friend to gather a good set of dialogue ideas to draw on when you demonstrate in front of the class.

Once this is working with the class, there are various refinements you can add. For example, look for the main quality in each character and see whether this can be reflected in their speech.

The fishermen might be cautious, the hunter might be impatient or angry, the mother might be mocking or loving.

Writing options

Mini play script; dialogue paragraph; poems.

Character profile

Imagine that one of the characters is introducing themselves at, say, a job interview. Show how this might be done for *The Freedom Song* with likes and dislikes, strengths and weaknesses, and other characteristics. For example:

'Hello. I am a hunter and I live in a little village in the middle of a big forest. I like shooting things with my bow and arrow and hate it when I miss. I'm really strong and fast and good at catching things, but not so great when I don't get my own way. I'm a bit impatient and get cross easily.'

Hear a few for each character in the story.

Writing options

Fill in a job application form; write an obituary.

Hot seat

This game is very popular and encourages questions that help to develop the character in ways that are relevant to the story. These might be questions about the character's home (basic details), how they felt at a particular moment, what they thought, what they saw, heard, smelt, what they learned from the experience, what they would have done differently and so on. These kinds of plot-related questions provide an excellent starting-point.

Basic method

First take the hot seat and demonstrate how to embody a character and take questions from the audience. Use a particular posture and voice for your character. Next ask a volunteer to take the hot seat and demonstrate asking the kinds of questions you'd like your students to ask.

Then open it up to the audience. At the end, ask the class what they would now add to the story and why. If the hot-seater gets stuck you might then open the question up to the floor for suggested answers.

Re-enactment

This activity involves the whole class in a retelling, and is fast, easy and fun. It doesn't need any planning. You can sit the class in a circle, explain that this is the stage space, and start to tell the story. Whenever you need a character or an object you will take a volunteer to become that thing or person on the stage. If speech is needed you will ask for it, otherwise they should stay silent. The storyteller (you) is the director and is in charge. They should follow instructions. For example:

'Once upon a time there was forest,'
(ask three people to be trees)

'One day a hunter was walking though the forest,'
(get the hunter to walk for a bit)

'when he came to a tree with a bird on the top.'
(ask for a volunteer to be the bird)

'The hunter thought,'
(get the hunter to speak praise of the bird)

'... and walked away.'

'Just then the bird pushed back its wings, poked out its beak, and sang down to the hunter ...'

And so on. Remember to send actors off the stage when they are no longer needed.

Variants

Find a student to be the storyteller and director and help them when needed.

Use mime only.

Divide up and rehearse in groups of seven, using the same method, then ask them to act back to the whole class for appreciation.

Stop the story from time to time and get ideas from the class on dialogue for the characters or things they might do.

Poems and pictures

Using poems and pictures can be a good way to demonstrate heightened use of language for storytelling. It can also be used to practise descriptions of various kinds.

1. Divide the story up into 15 moments on your story map.

2. Divide the class into 15 pairs and give a moment to each pair.

3. Get them to draw a time frozen sketch of that moment (in 5 minutes).

4. Visit another pair and ask them to talk about one another's pictures using who, what, where questioning to discover words for what was seen, heard, smelt and felt at that moment.

5. Now demonstrate how to write a quick 14- word poem, in 3 word, 4 word, 3 word, 4 word pattern. Here's an example for the moment when the hunter shoots the bird:

   Arrow through heart
   Bird bleeding, falling fast
   Thinks good shot!
   That serves him right!

6. Get every group to make a mini poem to go with their picture.

7. Now go round in the circle hearing each poem in narrative order. Then take them and re-read them in your voice. This can be quite powerful.

8. Feedback: choose favourite words and ideas students might use when they tell the story. If you like you can exhibit the pictures and poems in order on the wall.

Thought corridor

Choose a character and a moment in the story. Have two lines of students and a volunteer in character to walk down between them. As the character walks past, students call out what the character might be feeling or thinking. For example, at the moment when the hunter sees 100 birds on the tree:

What was he feeling?

Nervous, delighted, confused, thoughtful, excited ...

and so on

What was he thinking?

'That reminds me of something...'

'Will I never get rid of those wretched birds?'

'Didn't my mother tell me something about this?'

'Where is my bird book?'

and so on.

Variant

Choose a dilemma that occurs in the story, perhaps whether or not the hunter should shoot the bird at the beginning. As the character walks through the corridor, one side of the line can call out arguments in favour of the action, the other side, arguments against. Afterwards, feed back which ideas you might use in your story.

Feelings check-in

Re-enact the story, but pause in a freeze frame every now and then for a feelings check-in. Tap each frozen actor on the head and ask them to say what they are feeling and/or thinking at that moment in the plot. If actors get stuck you can take suggestions from the audience to help them to continue.

Variant

The same idea can be used with storytelling. Work in small groups with one storyteller, say, and three listeners. Listeners can clap any time to stop the story. The storyteller can then say what the character is feeling and thinking at that moment.

Radio or TV interview

Imagine a radio or TV interview is taking place with one of the characters. Role-play the interview in pairs, or have a press conference with the whole class. If needed, first talk about what kinds of questions will be interesting for the story (such as action, feeling, thinking, learning). You can also video the interviews for added excitement.

Writing option

A newspaper article.

Phone call role-play

Imagine that the character is calling a friend or relative and talking to them about what has happened. Demonstrate this with some interesting questions. Afterwards, role-play in pairs and re-enact to the group. Discuss what the best questions were and think about what could be added to the story.

Cartoon

Make a cartoon strip for the story, with narrator voice and speech bubbles. Each individual can use the whole story or be assigned a story section. Demonstrate options for perspectives, zooming and feeling evocation, or show examples from a graphic novel. It can be helpful to give templates for the characters that are easy to draw, so that they can be copied.

Paintings

Give each pair a story moment and have them create a painting, collage, or another kind of two-dimensional artwork. These can then be used to create a walk-through exhibition with guides to explain the story to visitors. Parents can be invited to view the exhibition.

Script

Assign a story section to each student or pair and ask them to write a small drama script to be enacted back to the class.

Screenplay

Create a storyboard of the story with instructions for the camera on how the film will look and sound.

Audio and video retelling

Tell the story into a microphone or camera. Recordings can be taken home as a good memory, or uploaded onto the school website (with all relevant permissions).

Tell or teach to others

Visit another class and set up small story circles with, say, two storytellers and two listeners. The storytellers tell the story to the listeners, and then ask them for their favourite moments, and so on. This is a great way to develop the story. Repeat for several classes and review with whole class after each telling to highlight problems and to discover things they have learnt. The experience of being a storyteller in public, outside the classroom, can be very powerful. Alternatively, pairs from one class could teach the story to a pair from another class, passing the story on.

Tell at home

Send the story map home with a note saying something like:

'This is a story map that your child has made of a story they are learning. Please ask them to tell you the story at least once, and then fill in this form with any comments about the experience of listening to it. Thanks!'

This involves parents and has been extremely popular in some schools.

Mime

Develop a mime piece, accompanied either by a narrator or perhaps short pieces of music, chosen by the students, that fit with each mood and create a whole performance.

Dance and movement

Extend a mimed piece to follow the rhythms and moods of the music and you will find you have dance. It can be in any style that the students choose.

Rap

Stories are easy to retell in rap style. You'll need to be able to demonstrate it yourself, unless you

have a good rapper in your class! You could learn one from the *Rapping Rats* book (see Sources and resources, p.155) if you can get it. *The Princess and the Pea* rap is quite a good place to start. Invent some movements to go with the rap and it can be a communal chant.

Reflecting circle

Don't forget to use your reflecting circles to play with fragments of the story using gesture and sound (see Chapter 3). In brief, make a circle and echo back fragments of the story, either as character or narrator, using sound, speech and gesture.

Story exhibition

Make a collection of pictures, objects and clips that can retell the story step-by-step and then assemble them into a story trail with labels for each section, so that visitors can walk through the story and have it told to them by story guides. These objects can be as simple as a picture of a tree, a bow and arrow, an audio clip of a song, an arrow in a toy bird, a bag, a table, feathers, a knife, a pot, and so on. An exhibition can generate lots of enthusiasm and parent involvement. The whole school can visit.

Playground mural

Paint pictures of each story step and then either frame them for outside use or paint them onto a school wall. Have guides available at playtime and after school to retell the story.

Story song

Compose a song of the story and teach it to the school in assembly.

So, these are 23 ideas to get the story growing and evolving with your class. Try them out and then invent your own or, better still, get your class to invent other games and exercises themselves.

Introducing basic plots and characters

Although every story is unique, there are some common patterns and conventions for creating plots and characters that can help students develop ideas for storytelling and writing. Some Storytelling Schools teach these patterns explicitly from Year 1 to Year 6, so that students are able to recognise basic characters and plots when they see them and also use those conventions in their own storymaking. Some teachers make little posters of the plots and characters and have them on display in their classroom for reference whenever discussing stories.

Our plots are based on those described in Christopher Booker's inspirational book *The Seven Basic Plots: Why We Tell Stories.*

The magnificent seven are:

1. Overcoming the monster
2. Rags to riches
3. Voyage and return
4. Quest
5. Comedy
6. Tragedy
7. Rebirth

We often focus on the following nine characters:

1. Heroes and heroines
2. Villains
3. Helpers
4. Mentors
5. Gatekeepers
6. Transformers
7. Shape shifters
8. Tricksters
9. Guardians

Whenever you teach a story, take a few minutes to review the type of story and the characters in it. You might do this after a story has been heard, after it has been learned or as part of the deepening stage of learning, and you can also do it with stories the class is reading. Done regularly, this will become a natural part of the class routine and is a great way of beginning to think about how plots work. Then, when you teach innovation and invention, the students will draw on this knowledge to create their own stories.

How you teach this depends on the age and aptitude of the students: here's one way to do it.

Seven basic plots

The first time you do this with KS2 you might want to present the idea of the seven plots to the class, and have them classify stories they know into one or more of the groups. For example, for a KS2 class you might explain that there are seven kinds of stories, each with their own particular plot. For KS1 you might start with the themes of voyage and return and rags to riches. Many stories fit into one or more of these story types, as shown in the table opposite.

You might then get the class to brainstorm examples of stories they know for each group from traditional stories, books, movies or any other source. Some examples are shown opposite.

It is clear from this list that many stories can be fitted into more than one of these categories. This is fine, and all part of the learning process for the students. You might like to make your own list of the stories known to your class. You could also map and step the seven plots themselves. Once the class has grasped the general idea of basic plots, you apply it every time a story is encountered.

Seven basic plots: summary

Story type	Basic Idea
1. Overcoming the monster	A monster or powerful, evil figure dominates the world of the story and must be defeated.
2. Rags to riches	A sympathetic, impressive hero in poor circumstances finds riches and happiness.
3. Voyage and return	A journey story, where the character has various adventures, often away from home, and gets home safely.
4. Quest	A journey story where the 'calling' of the main character is driven by a clear, imperative desire or task.
5. Comedy	Cases of mistaken identity and meanings lead to confusion for the characters within the story. The audience views unfolding events with a knowing eye.
6. Tragedy	The character flaws of the hero persist, causing pain and suffering.
7. Rebirth	Characters are 'reborn' – transformed with new attitudes and inclinations, following 'learning'.

Examples of the seven basic plots:

Story type	Examples
1. Overcoming the monster	*Minotaur, Beowulf, Jack and Beanstalk, Little Red Riding Hood, James Bond, David and Goliath, Jaws, Three Little Pigs* (if they live), *Bluebeard*
2. Rags to riches	*Cinderella, Puss in Boots, Aladdin, David Copperfield*
3. Voyage and return	*Alice's Adventures in Wonderland, The Chronicles of Narnia, Goldilocks, The Hobbit*
4. Quest	*Theseus, Perseus, The Lord of the Rings*
5. Comedy	*Lazy Jack, The Emperor's New Clothes*
6. Tragedy	*Icarus, Little Red Riding Hood* (if she dies), *The Boy Who Cried Wolf*
7. Rebirth	*Sleeping Beauty, The Ugly Duckling, Beauty and the Beast, Snow White, Thumbelina, The Very Hungry Caterpillar*

Story map books

In some Storytelling Schools, pupils stick all their story maps into a book to take with them on their journey through the school. These books function not only as a record of their storytelling repertoire but as a prompt that they can refer to when stories are revisited. As they acquire a bank of stories, pupils will also be starting to recognise similarities between them. When all the staff involved in a storytelling school activity use the seven basic plots as a shared reference, pupils will be able to say which stories are *Voyage and return* and which are *Quests*, and so on, in whatever context story is being discussed.

Wider applications

The opportunities for using this knowledge of plots when reflecting on stories are numerous and wide-ranging. They can occur following reading in all contexts, but the theory also applies to cartoons and films, stories from home, events at school and beyond, biographical stories in history and so on. It is important to recognise and point out to our pupils that all of these seven plots have applications in non-fiction and in our everyday lives. Perhaps we all have our own *overcoming the monster* story to deal with, whether it is an OFSTED inspection or a fear of interviews. Could the purchase of a lottery ticket have a *rags to riches* outcome? Every day, on the way to school or work, or just popping down to the shops, we all embark on our own *voyage and return* narratives. Our life experiences lead to a constant cycle of *rebirth* as we are shaped and changed by them. Driven by a sense that the grass is always somehow greener somewhere else we all, from time to time, embark on a personal *quest* to go somewhere or get our hands on some amazing gadget, or try to remove whatever stands between us and our perceived view of happiness. And while these five plots are playing out, misunderstandings may occur that can lead to some *comic* stories, while we do our best to avoid the *tragedies* our mistakes might bring us. Fictional stories, as well as the characters and their functions within them, reflect real life.

Nine basic character types

Students also need to become accustomed to recognising stock characters in the stories they encounter (see the 'character type' table on page 56). Just as with plots, you can introduce these characters to the class in one session and then refer to them whenever a new story is encountered. Characters often have more than one of the personality traits shown in the chart on page 56. Some schools have a permanent reminder of these traits on the classroom walls One key character type is 'the Trickster'.

Teaching about characters

The story of *Anansi and the Tiger* is a good way of introducing the trickster character in the form of a spider. When the class have heard the story, talk to them about Anansi. What is he like? Is he trustworthy? Is he kind? Is he clever? Does he lie? Explain that he is a trickster character who plays tricks to get what he wants. To reinforce the idea, you can get them to invent different kinds of tricks for Anansi to play in a new story. Perhaps he has to get a bone from a dog, gold from a dragon and a ride on a serpent's back. How would he do that?

You can listen to *Anansi and the Tiger* on the Story Museum website: **www.storymuseum.org. uk/1001stories**

Collect ideas and make up some stories. Next, students might make up their own Anansi story with different challenges and tricks. All can be mapped, stepped and retold. We will return to these concepts when we come to story invention in Chapter 7.

Anansi and the Tiger

Once upon a time there was a spider called Anansi. Now, it happened to be that all the stories told in that place were called Tiger stories. There was Tiger and Elephant, Tiger the Great and so on. Tiger simply knew and had all the best stories. Fed up with the situation, Anansi decided he would trick Tiger out of all his stories. Anansi went to Tiger's cave. 'Oh Tiger,' he called in a sing-song voice. Tiger came prowling out of his cave and growled. 'What do you want?'

'I've come to make you a deal,' said Anansi. 'I'll get you two things that you really want and in return you must give me all your stories.' Tiger was fed up with Anansi and thought this was a chance to get rid of him.

'Go and get me a barrel full of bees,' he told Anansi, 'And after that, a python.'

The deal was made. Anansi went to the beehive. 'Oh bees,' he sang.

The Queen Bee came out. 'Is it true that you bees squabble all the time?' 'No,' said the Queen Bee, 'We work as a team.'

'Prove it,' said Anansi, holding up an empty barrel, 'Show me how you can organise your bees to all get inside this pot.' The bees flew in and Anansi slammed down the lid. Next, Anansi went to Python. 'Is it true,' said Anansi, 'that cobra is the longest snake?' 'No', said Python, 'It's me.'

'Prove it,' said Anansi, holding out a long stick. 'Cobra is as long as this stick.' Python measured herself against the stick but she fell some way short.

'Let me tie your tail to the end of the stick,' said Anansi, 'Then you can stretch your neck out and show that you really are the longest snake.'

Anansi did this but Python still fell short. 'Let me tie your body to the middle of the stick,' said Anansi, 'then you can really stretch your head out.' With Python tied in the middle, Anansi then grabbed Python's neck and tied it to the stick. Anansi took Python and the bees back to Tiger who had to give Anansi all his stories.

This is why, if you ever go to that place, you will never find Tiger or any of his stories. From that day to this, all the stories belonged to Anansi.

Character types and their qualities

Character type	Qualities
1. Heroes and heroines	Usually the central characters in a story. They are often driven by events leading to a calling or quest. Heroes can have a variety of traits: being willing, unwilling, a loner, group-orientated, an anti-hero (outsider) are typical of many.
2. Villains	Usually the enemy of the hero, and often the most significant obstacle to be overcome. Villains' wants may be fuelled by greed or hate, and will harm others. They often have a weakness, such as sunlight or water in the case of witches, or arrogance that leads to their downfall.
3. Helpers	Help the heroes achieve their aims. Often stumbled upon accidentally. Helpers may become active when the hero first helps them. They can provide gifts of magic, advice or directly intervene to save the hero.
4. Mentors	Particular kinds of helper who provide ongoing wisdom to the hero.
5. Gatekeepers	Guard the doorway from one place to another. They need to be befriended or overcome on the hero's journey.
6. Transformers	Change identity, while keeping the same physical shape.
7. Shape shifters	Can change from one physical form to another.
8. Tricksters	These characters are good at playing tricks, deceiving or cheating in various ways. They may help or hinder the hero or be the main story character.
9. Guardians	Their function is to look after something and protect it. May be helpful or an obstacle to the hero.

Chapter 6

Innovation

What is innovation?

The previous chapters described how to learn a story and develop it, deepening character, description, dialogue and drama while keeping the main elements basically the same. The story's setting, characters, dilemmas and resolutions remain similar, but the way that they are conveyed is developed. In this chapter, we explore innovation, where the intention is to *change* main elements in the story. The plot structure stays basically the same but the plot *content* is changed. This may be as simple as changing the name of a character or type of animal, or it may involve completely changing the setting, characters and dilemma of the story within the same plot format.

We will describe three ways to innovate:

➤ substitution;

➤ addition;

➤ plot recycling.

Changing stories

During the imitation stage, students learn language patterns within a particular story.

In innovation, they learn to reapply those patterns in different ways, increasing their level of mastery in their use. In this way innovation is a stepping-stone towards full invention where whole new stories are created. It allows them to experiment with changing stories and seeing what happens. Doing this involves *generating* ideas, *reflecting* on the quality of the ideas and

deciding which ideas to use in the story. This sequence is a basic requirement for learning and critical thinking.

The process of innovation moves us into story making: beginning to make up new things and seeing how to fit them together into a story. This involves developing a sense of what plot is and how it works. Best of all, innovation can be loads of fun. Normally, a class will learn to tell and deepen a story before moving to this stage. Now they have freedom to play with the story, using ideas they find interesting and exciting. They have a chance to add in things that they really like.

Often when teaching innovation, we will say something like, 'OK, you know the story, now we're going to change it and add new things that *you really love*, things that you care about.' This can create huge joy. Football lovers can add their football heroes, pet lovers can add their favourite animals, video gamers add their favourite battles and dragon-lovers add their favourite dragons. Just being given permission to add something that you really love to a story can be empowering. Your own likes and experiences are affirmed.

We were once retelling *Little Red Riding Hood* with a class. One boy loved wrestling and wanted to retell the story with a wrestling theme. When he made his suggestion to the class we could feel he was making a challenge, expecting to be told to find a 'better' subject. When we welcomed his idea and helped develop it he was absolutely delighted and created quite a complex and subtle story. The teacher was amazed and so was he.

The key was to allow him to follow what he loved. That's the great thing about innovation – you've got a great plot already, so great new stories can happen without having to create one from scratch.

Innovation also offers the chance to explore personal issues on a metaphorical and often unconscious level. When we start making up stories we often bring in personal motifs and concerns. In another group, a child was telling an innovation story about animals defecating all over the place. Again, he expected to be told off and told to choose a 'good' subject. Instead we accepted the idea and asked him what was the real problem that these animals were dealing with. The child replied that animals in the house were being hurt and they were trying to escape. It was a spine-tingling moment as we realised that the child might be exploring his own situation through the story.

Innovation also teaches us that stories can change. This can be quite a revelation for students who get attached to a single version as the 'right' one. Trial and error is fine, as we keep some ideas and drop others. One of the advantages about doing this orally is that you don't have to write anything down. It's really quick and easy to try something and change it.

If you don't like it then try something else. Writing takes much longer and things can feel much harder to change once they are down on paper.

It's usually best to demonstrate an aspect of innovation first with the whole class, collecting plenty of suggestions for changes, so that students who have an initial blank when asked for ideas can simply choose someone else's idea to get them started. That way everyone in the class can have a sense of inclusion and autonomy.

One way to start thinking about innovation is with the plot matrix. We can change things in any of these boxes, remembering that changes in one box will often have consequences for others.

The plot matrix

1 Where (setting)	2 Who (character)	3 What (problem/want/need/dilemma)
4 Obstacle(s)	5 Setback(s)	6 Helper
7 Solution (resolution of main problem)	8 Ending (how do we leave the story?)	9 Learning (lessons, moral for characters, storyteller and audience)

Take *The Freedom Song,* for example. Some things could be changed without much consequence, such as:

Character

➤ the hunter could become a teacher, or a footballer

➤ he could become a she

➤ the fishermen could be kids swimming in the river

Obstacle

➤ the bubbling pot could become a hot oven

➤ the bird could get put in a fridge during the cooking sequence

Setting

➤ the whole thing could be set in a town

Learning

➤ there could be a new learning at the end, for example,
'If you can't change it then you'd better get used to it.'

Ending

➤ there could be a new ending, for example the hunter could go to his mother who tells him all about the Freedom Bird

Chapter 6 Innovation

In all of these examples the new ideas can be added without having to make big changes to the rest of the story.

However, there are other changes that will have consequences for retelling that the storymaker needs to think about. For example:

➤ if the bird becomes a dog, the puppies will have to jump out of the box, not fly, and they might have to bark rather than sing. The ending might change too: the barking might just stop once the hunter has made friends with the puppies

➤ if the bird was roasted in the oven, not chopped, the 100 animals moment that occurs when the box is opened might be lost, which could weaken the story

➤ if the hunter had a friend with him then a whole strand of dialogue could be developed throughout the whole story

➤ if the story happened on the moon with astro-nauts then we'd have to think of an annoying moon creature that fitted into that world

We need to demonstrate to our students the fun of having all sorts of new ideas, trying them out, deciding what works and choosing a favourite idea. If you enjoy innovating yourself, you will inspire your students to follow suit.

How to teach innovation

Substitution

A simple substitution involves making a few changes such as altering a character, setting or objects in a story. You will have to calibrate the basic approach depending on the age and aptitude of your class. Here's an example:

➤ Say something like,
'Now we are going to change things in the story: let's brainstorm ideas for ways to change the hunter and the bird. What could they be instead?'

➤ Take lots of ideas and then point out problems to solve. For example, if the main character works as a teacher then why would he or she have a weapon to kill the bird? Or if the bird becomes a frog how would the frog climb a tree? And so on.

➤ Then let pairs go away and choose a few changes and tell them back to the class in their own way. Discuss favourite changes and what works well, and what didn't quite fit with the story. If needed the students can remap and step the new story.

You can also use pictures to give ideas for additions. For example, you might choose a story with an animal character and then show some pictures of various animals. Ask each student to choose one animal to be their character. You could repeat this for setting and key objects. For some, a picture can trigger lots of new ideas.

It can be helpful to give examples of substitutions first to give the class the idea.

Additions

Here we can add new things into the story. These could be in the form of speech, description or narration. For example, adding:

➤ a description of the forest at the beginning of the story.

➤ a more detailed description of the house where the hunter lives.

➤ new phrases or dialogue that the hunter might say to himself. For example:
'Why, oh why, do I have to hear this annoying sound?'

➤ a new character. For example, the hunter might go through the whole story with a friend and have a conversation with them at each stage.

➤ a song or mini poem. For example, the Freedom Bird might sing a song with the words:
'Freedom, freedom, freedom is what I love.'

➤ or the hunter can have a little chant or phrase at every step, like:

'That sound is making me feel bad. If I don't stop it I'll go mad!'

> new things that the character interacts with in the story. For example, the bird could be put in a cupboard, then in the fridge, then chopped up and put in the oven, then put on a plate to eat, before sending it off down the river.

> completely new incidents. For example, the hunter might chat with his mother after the bird floats away and she might give him some advice.

In short, there are all sorts of things that you can add to change the story around. In general, you will probably want to demonstrate one or more examples, ask for suggestions and then listen to retellings of the story with the new features. Then give the audience an opportunity to practise critical reflection by asking them to talk about their favourite changes and why they worked.

Recycle the whole plot

When the class is ready, they can experiment with changing everything in a story while keeping the same plot. Here is one way to teach this for *The Freedom Song*:

Start by outlining that this is a story about something annoying that just won't stop whatever the character tries, until finally the character accepts that it is here to stay.

Point out the main steps in the plot as follows:

1. Where?
2. Who?
3. Problem (something annoying)
4. First try to stop it
5. Second try to stop it
6. Third try to stop it
7. Ending (acceptance)

Now start brainstorming ideas for the various columns in the table below. Try starting with the problem. Ask the students to give ideas for annoying things they would like to have in the story. You can prompt them to think of things that really annoy them.

Examples could be: footballers cheating, playground bullies, a bossy teacher, spiders in the bed, a moaning little sister.

Now ask pairs to choose one of the problems and think of characters and a setting to go with it. Chart these up on the board.

The football story could have a goalie getting more and more fed up with losing because the opposition dives and gets penalties in every match. The bully could be in the playground always picking on the main character. The bossy teacher would keep on shouting at a child. The moaning little sister at home just wouldn't be quiet.

Chart up all these ideas then ask each group to think of three ways in which their characters could fail to stop the thing that is annoying them and then learn how to live with it.

Finally the groups can choose a new storyline, step it and tell it and maybe do some story deepening with their new versions.

Table for brainstorming innovations:

Where?	Who?	Problem	First try	Second try	Third try	Ending
Playground	Bully and victim	Bullying	Ask them nicely to stop	Fight back	Give sweets	Group support

Chapter 7

Invention

Creating new stories

In previous chapters we looked at how to learn and retell a story and then how to innovate by changing some or all of the story elements while retaining the same basic plot.

Now, we are going to explore invention: how to teach your class to make up new stories. We'll explain various ways of doing this including:

➤ invention from a basic plot;

➤ invention from character;

➤ invention with objects;

➤ invention with pictures;

➤ invention with plot matrix.

We'll also demonstrate some ways of refining story ideas as they emerge.

What is invention?

Nobody can be quite sure where innovation ends and invention begins. When it comes to storytelling the three I's – imitation, innovation and invention – are all part of a single continuum, moving from memorised repetition at one extreme to free and spontaneous improvisation at the other. As teachers, we need to walk our pupils, step by step, along that continuum.

For the purposes of this handbook, invention means creating a new story without reference to a particular known story. Creating a story about

defeating a monster is invention. Rewriting *Theseus and the Minotaur* with a new setting and characters but the same detailed plot we call innovation. In the classroom, we are innovating when we teach a story then change it. With invention, we start from scratch without a particular story in mind. This is a creative process. Some see the ability to create new stories as an innate quality possessed by only a few people. We'd like to challenge that. We believe that story invention is a learnable skill.

The first thing to bear in mind is that, consciously or subconsciously, we make up new stories from the ones we know already, splicing and matching pieces of them together in different ways. The stories that provide our raw material may be ones we have heard or read, they may be from fiction or real life. This means that, as teachers, if we want our students to invent new stories, we have to fill them with lots of great stories first. All the work in previous chapters has been part of developing our pupils' capacity to invent.

Secondly, many of the skills that we developed when learning imitation and innovation are also used in invention. When we learn a story to tell, we often build up characters and a sense of place. We then create significant dilemmas that evolve into a satisfying resolution. When we start changing parts of a known story, we learn to reflect on how changing one story element may affect the others. We need all of these skills when inventing stories.

The plot matrix, discussed in Chapter 6, is one way to think about this.

1 Where?	2 Who?	3 What?
Setting	Character	Problem/want/ need/dilemma
4 Obstacle(s)	**5 Setback(s)**	**6 Helper** or other new character
7 Solution Resolution of main problem?	**8 Ending** How do we leave the story?	**9 Learning** Lessons, moral for characters, storyteller and audience

A third principle, running through the whole handbook, is that in order to teach something we need to demonstrate how to do it before asking our students to have a go. When it comes to developing stories there are three stages:

➤ generative – coming up with ideas;

➤ reflective – thinking about the ideas and which have merit;

➤ selective – choosing which ones to keep.

As teachers, we first have to learn the process of invention, at least to a standard where we can demonstrate these stages to our class. This helps us to understand our pupils' learning process and enables us to be a role model for them.

We describe a number of ways of inventing stories. Each provides a different frame to help students generate, review and select ideas for their stories.

Warm-ups

If you have not yet read Chapter 3, please do so. It is full of warm-up games that help students to practise spontaneous invention. 'Tell me more', object games, picture games, copying games and fortunately-unfortunately are all great ways to get story ideas going. Many of these warm-ups generate ideas that can be developed into wonderful stories that can be mapped, stepped, retold and written. The games model a playfulness that really helps to get creative ideas to flow.

'Spontaneous' invention

The purest form of invention is simply making up a new story, then developing and refining it. There are an infinite number of ways to do this, using a particular stimulus to get the story going. This may be a word, title, object, picture, memory, or anything that can suggest an idea for a story.

In a storytelling classroom, your students will need to regularly practise simply 'making up a story'. You can leave it up to them how they do it. They will naturally draw on and apply their existing knowledge of language, plot and character to create stories. It is important for them to apply what they know. You just need to name the telling aim (if any) and let the individuals, pairs and groups create a story for telling. Stimulus you could offer might be:

➤ A title

➤ An object

➤ A picture

➤ A sound

➤ A memory

➤ A sentence

➤ A poem

You might suggest a genre, mood or style to aim for, such as:

➤ Killing the monster

➤ Voyage and return

➤ Thriller

➤ Horror

➤ War

➤ Romance

or you could choose a historical period, such as:

➤ The Normans

➤ The Tudors

➤ World War I

Whatever you choose to use, make sure you give your groups time to work out and develop the idea. You can then hear the stories as a class and practise appreciative and critical listening, so that 'first draft' stories can be improved. Once this is done, the stories can be mapped, stepped and retold, and, if desired, written down. Make this a regular part of your storytelling classroom.

Invention from a basic plot

Now it is time to apply the idea of the seven basic plots, discussed in Chapter 4, and our suggestion that whenever a story is learned, whether told, read or watched, there can be a discussion with the class about the basic plot type a story fits into. To recap, these plots are:

➤ Overcoming the monster

➤ Rags to riches

➤ Voyage and return

➤ Quest

➤ Comedy

➤ Tragedy

➤ Rebirth

For example: *Cinderella* is a rags to riches story, *Theseus and the Minotaur* is an overcoming the monster story, and so on. In this way, you can familiarise your class with the seven plots as a regular routine. Once your class is familiar with at least one of these plots you can start inventing new stories on the same theme. You can do it in a similar way to the 'plot recycling' method in Chapter 6, using general plot guidelines to work from. The chart on page 64 sets out a useful set of plot summaries.

Basic Plots

PLOT	Where?	Who?	What problem?	Resolution/ Ending	Learning
Overcoming the monster	Place suffering from monster	Hero	Evil monster causes suffering	Monster over-come or killed	Courage Perseverance Cleverness
Rags to riches	Humble home	Poor, likeable individual	Oppressed, victimised, poor and unfulfilled hero	Emancipated, empowered, rich and happy hero	Kindness Cleverness Fairness
Voyage and return	Familiar home and unfamiliar new place	Explorer	How to survive and return from new land	Creation of home with new qualities	Courage Understanding
Quest	Anywhere	Hero	Particular goal, often with reward	Goals achieved, much learned	Courage
Comedy	Anywhere	Fools	Misunderstandings	The moment of realisation (or not)	Understanding
Tragedy	Anywhere	Flawed protago-nist	A calling or goal that will deliver personal pain	Unsatisfactory outcome for protagonist	Consequences of flaw
Rebirth	Anywhere	Anyone	Something causing unhappiness – often self-imposed	Transformed	Perspective radically changed

Illustration

This is one way to create a story with your class, using a basic plot as a starting point, in this case 'voyage and return'. Start by reminding your class about the main elements in a voyage and return story, then brainstorm ideas in a grid with the class, which might include:

Home	Unfamiliar place	Mode of travel	Explorer character	Threats	Solutions	Endings

You might think of unfamiliar places to travel to and possible threats to encounter there. For example:

➤ icebergs, polar bears and the cold in the Arctic;

➤ lions, snakes and swamps in the jungle;

➤ aliens, warriors, moon monsters and faulty equipment on a moon journey;

➤ sharks, whales and man-eating seaweed in the deep ocean;

➤ cheats, hooligans and sickness at an away football match.

Or you might think of characters first and what hazardous journeys they might make:

➤ a child might journey to school alone, facing dangerous roads, angry bullies and a complicated bus timetable;

➤ a dog might travel across the city and back to visit his old home, facing cats, rats and dog catchers;

➤ a rat might travel through the sewers to look for some fun;

➤ a flea might travel onto a new dog and then back again.

Fill up the board with ideas then get each child or group to choose a story idea and fill in all the sections of the matrix. They can then pitch their story to the class for feedback. For example:

An explorer travels north to the Arctic to reach the North Pole. He travels on a sledge pulled by eight dogs. On the way, he travels over loose ice, falls in the water and nearly dies of cold; next he is attacked by a polar bear which eats four of his dogs; finally another traveller steals his sledge and he has to walk back home, catching fish to eat and sleeping in his tent at night.

For each story pitch let the class offer ideas for ways to make the story even better. As a teacher, you can lead by modelling key questions from the nine-step plot matrix (p. 62):

➤ what was his home like?

➤ what kind of person was he and why did he want to travel?

➤ how did he overcome the obstacles?

➤ what did he learn?

➤ what was it like when he came home?

and so on...

If your class gets good at this, they can offer feedback in small groups so that everyone gets a chance to pitch their idea. Then, when the students are ready, they can map, step and tell their stories in various ways using the methods described in Chapter 4.

Invention from a character

Character development is an essential part of creating any story. For a tale to work well, the audience must identify with the characters, caring about what happens to them. Without empathy with the characters, a story will fall flat. During the process of storytelling, deepening and innovating, your class will need to have worked with character development. Now, in the stage of invention these skills will be applied further. The exercises on character in Chapters 3, 4 and 6 can all be used to practise invention skills from characters.

Character-specific exercises described in previous chapters include:

➤ Tell me more (page 26)
➤ Cocktail party (page 32)
➤ Character reflecting (page 30)
➤ Character dialogue (page 47)
➤ Character profile (page 48)
➤ Hot seat (page 48)
➤ Interviews (page 50)
➤ Role-play (page 50)

Using stock characters

First we will look at choosing a stock story character and using this as a starting point for creating a story, then discuss ways to use any kind of character to build a story. Chapter 5 introduced the notion of teaching basic character types as a good preparation for story invention, suggesting that whenever you discuss a story with the class you use the opportunity to teach these character types.

1. Heroes and heroines

Usually the central character in a story, often driven by events leading to a 'calling' or quest. Heroes can have a variety of traits and responses to the quest: willing, unwilling, loner, group orientated, anti-hero (outsider) are typical.

2. Villains

Usually the enemy of the hero, and often the most significant obstacle they must overcome. Their wants may be fuelled by greed or hate, and will harm others. Often villains have a weakness or fatal flaw, e.g. sunlight, or water in the case of witches, or arrogance that leads to their downfall.

3. Helpers

Help the heroes achieve their aims. Often stumbled upon accidentally. Often helpers become active when the hero first helps them. Helpers can give gifts of magic, advice or directly intervene to save the hero.

4. Mentors

Particular kinds of helper who provide ongoing wisdom to the hero.

5. Gatekeepers

Guard the doorway from one place to another. They need to be befriended or overcome on the hero's journey.

6. Transformers

Change identity, while keeping the same physical shape.

7. Shape shifters

Transform from one physical form to another.

8. Tricksters

These characters are good at playing tricks, deceiving or cheating in various ways. They may help or hinder the hero or be the main story character.

9. Guardians

Function to look after something and protect it. May be helpful or an obstacle to our hero.

Let us give you an example of how to create a new story starting with a stock character. We will work with the villain. You may have introduced villains in previous lessons and may want to start with a reminder about the part they play in a story and collect examples from the class. Next, choose one and perhaps with a picture on the board list the key qualities of the known character. You could include name, appearance, habitat, wants, deeds, powers, and weaknesses. Shown here is the villain Baba Yaga from *Baba Yaga's Black Geese*.

You could then explain that wants, powers and weaknesses are essential to the villain character, so that it can be both threatening and ultimately defeatable. You can deepen connection with these characters using warm-up and deepening exercises from Chapters 3 and 5.

Now brainstorm some new villain characters with the class, using the same checklist of attributes as before. Your pupils can then invent their own villain using the checklist. You can add a few examples yourself if needed. Here are some suggestions:

Name	Appearance	Home	Wants	Powers and deeds	Weakness
Bonebreaker	Tough, short, muscled, always angry	Body building gym family	Glory	Breaks opponents' legs in football matches	Fear of spiders
Mr Scoff-face	Thin, cold-hearted, smells of blood	School	Revenge	Eats students for breakfast	Bad at house cleaning
Fireboy	Tall, red body, thin yellow eyes, hot to touch	Volcano	Excitement	Starts fires when bored	Fear of water
Spell woman	Purple cloak, pink fuzzy hair, black nail varnish and big boots	Beauty salon	Admiration	Magics spots and boils onto the faces of girls who make her jealous	Impulsive
Music woman	Electric bass, punk mohican, black leather gear, black lipstick and nails	Recording studio	Fame	When she plays music, it makes the listeners into slaves who do what she says without question and listen to no one else's music	Pride
Fox	Smooth, sleek, shiny and smart	Foxhole	Food	Speed, sharp teeth, patience	Greed

When you have a board full of ideas, talk about the ones that seem to work well. Start to imagine how a particular weakness might create a good story. For example, the hero takes spiders onto the pitch in his pocket, the teacher is discovered by following trails of blood, Fireboy is lured into a carwash and captured, and so on. When they are ready, have individuals or groups think up a story idea, either based on ideas from the board or using a brand new idea. Ask them to pitch their ideas, then map, step and tell.

Using new characters

You can use a similar exercise where the student is free to make up any character as a starting point for a new story. This might come from an exercise like 'Tell me more (lies)' (p. 28) or the stories from the everyday objects game (p. 28) or just ask each student or group to brainstorm completely new character ideas using a set of standard prompts like:

➤ Name

➤ Appearance

➤ Home

➤ Friends and relatives

➤ Strengths and weaknesses

➤ Hopes and fears

➤ Main problem

You could demonstrate this for everyday characters, magical characters, animal characters, or just leave it open. Then continue as with the previous stock character exercises. Don't forget that in all character work, body and voice games are an excellent way to get into the mood of the character. If things go a bit flat, get the class on their feet and have them become the characters for a while.

It is important to learn to identify things that work well in building character and story. Take plenty of time for a class review of student ideas throughout the invention process. Remember it is the learning that is important, not just the story!

Using a picture of a character

A picture or photograph of potential characters is another way to stimulate invention. This can be demonstrated to your class before asking them to invent their own idea.

First show them a picture and discuss ideas about who the character is. Prompts might include:

What is their name?

How old are they?

Where do they live?

Where were they born?

Have they got any friends and family?

What are their key characteristics?

Have they got any secrets?

And so on.

Choose a set of ideas for a character and then move on to questions to begin to draw out a narrative:

What do they want?

What obstacles stand in their way?

How do they overcome these obstacles?

From this list of questions, discuss possible answers and feel your way into a story perhaps based on one of the seven basic plots. You might decide early on that a tragedy would work well. Once you have made a decision, you can shape your answers to the above questions. This is a story told us by a Year 5 pupil:

The old lady in the picture was called Rebecca Howes. She was nicknamed Mother Goose because she was very snappy and protective of her family. Unfortunately, she tended to be over-protective, particularly of her youngest son, Charlie.

The family lived in a small cottage by a river but Charlie was never allowed to play near the river because Rebecca was worried about him drowning (no one in her family could swim). The river became a symbol of mystery to Charlie so much so, that one day he ignored his mum's warning and went to the river to play. He fell in. Rebecca rushed to help and managed to save Charlie, but drowned herself.

The story that pupil created is a tragedy. Once you know your answers, they can be made to fit any of the basic plots. Later, when you reflect upon your shared story, you can discuss as a class which questions worked best, which were specifically relevant to the particular picture or character that you used and which were stock questions. Once this has been demonstrated, let the students develop their own story idea from the picture using a similar set of prompts, pitch it to the class and then move to mapping, stepping and deepening, and perhaps into writing.

Invention with objects

Objects allow students to use both touch and sight to trigger ideas. You might like to make a collection of objects for your class to use, or ask them to bring some in themselves. One way to use the collection to generate stories is as follows:

Tell your pupils that they are going to use great questions to practise making up stories about objects. Here are some good questions to start with:

What is it?

How did you come by it?

Who made it?

Did it have any previous owners?

How your life changed since you got it? (e.g. good/bad luck/possible curses)

What magical powers does it have?

What do you want to do with your powers?

What adventures have you had with it?

You can vary the questions each time you explore invention in this way. You might then tell a story that you have made up yourself using an object and these questions. It can be helpful to begin by demonstrating the use of the first person voice ('I') as many students find it is easier to start that way.

For example, this prepared story uses a small, interesting box with four smooth pebbles inside as a starting point:

Last summer I was visiting my dad in Leicester when I found this box. My Dad said that he bought it many years ago from a bazaar in Egypt when he was travelling with the army. The old man who sold it to him said that it had once been owned by a king and made by the royal carpenter who was known to have magical powers. I tried to open the box but the lid was locked. I took the box home with me. After that, strange things started to happen. At night I would hear faint voices, 'Look to the bottom of the box', they said. I turned the box over and examined the four tiny legs. I found that when I turned all four of them to the left, the lid of the box opened. There, inside I found four tiny pebbles ...

Tell your story and then ask your pupils to reflect in pairs, saying 'What was the best bit of the story?' 'How could it have been better?' 'Was it believable?' and then, 'What questions do you think I asked myself when I was making it up?' Acknowledge your pupils' suggestions and then share the questions that you actually used. Read through the list of questions you have prepared on the board, reflecting on why each question is useful when making up a story about an object.

Next, you could encourage pupils to ask you the same questions about another object, and you could improvise a series of answers. These answers will begin to sound like a story. It will not yet be rounded or complete, but this does not matter because you are practising the core skill of the session: asking questions, reflecting on the answers and finally selecting which ideas to use.

Your pupils can then work in pairs with their own object, taking turns to interview each other using the prompts you have chosen. Explain that the person asking the questions and listening to the responses is the audience. Often, when students interview each other for the first time, someone will put up their hand very quickly to say 'We're finished.' At this point explain that the questions you offered as prompts were only the start. For example, to the first question 'How did you come by it?' the listener may just accept an answer such as 'I got it in a shop.' Reaffirm the point that the listener is the audience whose job is to help develop the story. Should the audience be satisfied with the response 'I got it in a shop'? Encourage students to think about the next question they are going to ask. This may have to be modelled, as in the following example:

Teacher: How did you come by it?

Child: I got it at the shops.

Teacher: Where was the shop? The person who sold it to you – what did they look like? Did they tell you anything about the object? Why were you attracted to the object in the first place?

The principle of reflecting upon the answer and deciding what the next question should be is very important. Discourage pupils from responding with 'I don't know' to any question. They should always try to come up with an answer. The Tell Me More game (pages 26 and 28) will help students to dig deeper into any answer. The class will also need several rotations, working with different partners as they develop their story idea. End the session with a few stories performed to the whole group with constructive feedback.

The outcome to these sessions can be some great stories told in the first person. You might want to map, step and speak them once the main idea is clear and then, if you like, move into story writing. Once your class has mastered invention in the first person, they can repeat the activity for third person storytelling using 'Once upon a time' story language.

Using the plot matrix

Another way to create a story is to use the nine-step plot matrix itself as a frame. The basic method is to work through the matrix, shown on the facing page, using appropriate questions to generate ideas for each section, and then refining the idea until it makes a credible story. You can start with any part of the matrix and then come up with ideas for other sections. For example, you might decide to invent a story about not being greedy, have an ending where someone loses all their friends, then have a greedy character in a school who steals everyone's sweets until they are found out. Or you might start with a problem about always getting lost and a resolution about learning how to read a map and then work from there.

A photocopiable version of the plot matrix appears on page 71 opposite.

The plot matrix

1 Where?	2 Who?	3 What?
4 Obstacle(s)?	**5 Setback(s)?**	**6 Helper** or other key character function
7 Solution	**8 Ending**	**9 Learning**

Before you ask your class to do this, demonstrate it on the board with the whole class. You can put a nine-step table up on the board like this:

1. Where?	2. Who?	3. What?	4. Obstacle(s)?	5. Setback(s)?	6. Helper	7. Solution	8. Ending	9. Learning

You might say,

'Let's think of some characters to create a story about. Who would you like to make up a story about?'

Say they choose:

'Dragon, footballer, teacher, princess and mouse'

These could go in the 'who?' column.

Then say

'OK let's choose one, dragon.'

Where does he live (cave, mountain, house...choose one, say cave)?

What problem does he face (is he hungry, bored, lonely? let's choose lonely)?

Obstacles: why is it difficult to overcome his loneliness? (has to guard gold so can't leave, and everyone is scared of him)

Helpers: his mum organises a dragon party for him in the cave.

Setback: he's so shy he runs away and the dragons steal all his gold.

Resolution: he gathers his courage, goes back to the party and dances with the dragons who really like his moves.

Ending: he starts making friends

Learning: even if you are shy you can make friends if you try.

Do this kind of thing for a few characters or settings and then have students do this alone or in pairs.

If students work alone, you can take them through this step-by-step in a kind of guided fantasy. Sometimes playing music can help. One approach is to give each student a sheet of paper with nine numbered boxes of the matrix, and talk them through it section by section, asking them to imagine a character, place, problem and so on, and then draw a little picture of each idea in the appropriate box. Doing this in silence can give real focus and let each student's imagination flow freely.

However, some classes may need the stimulus of a discussion for each section in the matrix. In this case, they can work in pairs or threes to develop an idea, again drawing pictures in each of the nine boxes to represent their story idea.

Once stories have been developed, they can be pitched to the whole class for feedback or review in small groups. Students can then map, step and deepen their stories before moving them into writing if desired.

Believability

In upper KS2 your pupils can begin to apply the concept of believability. This is important because stories need to be credible in order to work. The audience has to believe the story at the time of telling, however 'unrealistic' it is. The key question here is: 'Was the story believable within the world of the story?'

One way to teach this is to take an object or picture and place it at the centre of a large piece of sugar paper. Divide the page into four roughly equal areas around the image and label the paper like this:

Key questions	Facts/believable truths
Character biographies	Problems/resolution and final learning

The basic idea is to separate these four elements when planning a story, brainstorming, sifting and selecting ideas for each box before moving on to create a story. We need the following:

1. Key questions about the object of the story.

2. A biography of that main character, generated in the same way as for the painting of the old woman on page 68.

3. A set of credible ideas which make the story convincing.

4. A satisfactory resolution and learning.

This four-box matrix can be used in many ways to develop a story. Here's an example of how to teach students in this way, with a photograph of football boots as a starting point.

Show the picture to the class and explain it was taken a few years ago. Explain that the idea is to use the four-box matrix to make up a believable story with a mixture of facts and fiction:

Key questions

Ask the pupils to work with a partner to think of interesting questions related to this pair of shoes, made in 1922. As they volunteer their ideas, sort the questions into those that are general (good for any object), and those that are specific to these boots.

These specific questions are the 'key questions'. That's not to say that the other generic questions will not be important or even become key questions as we dig deeper into the emerging story, but questions like, 'Why are they red?' and 'Why do they look so new?' or 'Why does it look like they were never worn?' are useful to record under key questions because they are specific to the image and have the potential to trigger a narrative idea.

Believable truths

The next concept to model is the believability. To do this, present these 'facts' relating to the red shoes. They may or may not be true.

➤ These boots were made in Germany by Adolph Dassler in 1922.

➤ Adolf was an unpopular name in the last century for reasons the pupils may well surmise, so Adolph Dassler was known as 'Adi' Dassler. (Pupils get very excited when they make the connection themselves that these might have been the first pair of Adidas boots you could buy.)

➤ They cost five guineas (guinea = £1.05).

➤ Many amateur football players in 1922 still played in their everyday boots because they couldn't afford football boots.

➤ These boots belonged to Henry Trolley, the captain of Headington Football Club in 1922.

You could add 'facts' like Trolley was a greengrocer and so on, making up a few more 'believable truths' of your own. Once they have been presented, ask your pupils, 'What was true and what was false?' This simple question will stimulate a debate. Hopefully, both initially and after some scrutiny, all the above facts will sound believable to most pupils. In concluding this debate, you can then share with your pupils the fact that owner and maker of these boots are unknown. They may be a little surprised by this admission. You can ask them, 'But did the facts sound believable?' If so, you as a story inventor have just established a set of 'believable truths' that will help your new story sound convincing to any audience.

Once pupils become familiar with believability, story invention using history topics as a context becomes very exciting, because they can mould real facts as well as invented facts into believable truths.

Character biographies

This is the area of the planning sheet where pupils flesh out answers to generic questions about a character such as Henry Trolley, aged nineteen:

➤ lives in Headington;

➤ has a fiancée called Fran and is saving up for a house with her;

➤ works in his father's grocery store;

➤ earns five shillings a week;

➤ dreams of being the captain of his team, playing for England and becoming famous and rich. Wants these boots so badly, he's prepared to do anything!

➤ secretly starts stealing money from the family business and his 'house fund', and so on.

Problems

Next, brainstorm a list of problems relating to this shoe that might include things like:

➤ Henry couldn't afford the boots;

➤ five guineas were six months' wages for a greengrocer;

➤ only one shop in Oxford sold them and the boots were locked inside a glass case;

➤ the shop was well protected with staff and locks and the police station was next door.

The pupils might then decide that Henry stole the boots and would write this down in *Believable truths*. This could start a chain of thinking: How did he steal them? Perhaps he stole the money but from whom? Another character might start to appear in the Character Biography section of the planning sheet.

Perhaps Henry started to steal money from his father's greengrocer business. But, quite easily, the story can go other ways. Perhaps when talking about Henry, the pupils decide that he was honest and hardworking, character traits they would have noted in the Character Biographies. Then, perhaps Henry worked hard, taking on two extra jobs, working so hard that he became ill. He gets the boots, but loses his place on the team because he's had to take time off to recover, which explains why those boots never get worn. There are many possible outcomes. The thought process stimulated by this way of working can be exciting and free flowing.

Resolution and learning

Here the pupils can record the resolutions and learning that most appeal to them: Henry dies from overwork, taking on extra jobs to get the money for the boots. Henry's girlfriend falls out with him for stealing the money from their house deposit. Henry goes to prison – whatever it might be.

Reflecting and then selecting the idea

As with every activity in this chapter, the reflective and selective processes follow the generative. Once ideas start to fill up the sheet, it is time to reflect upon selecting the questions you really want to focus on. When modelling, start with the key questions and tick the ones that really grab you, with a double-tick for the most exciting one of all, for example 'Why were the boots never worn?' Then do the same with the problems and the learning and then again in the character biography box, ticking the key character traits that will need emphasis because of their importance to the narrative. It is also the point at which you decide on the basic plot. Once a plot begins to form, the pupils can map the sequence of events. They can then step and tell, rehearsing for their oral presentation.

After this has been demonstrated as a class activity, you can repeat it with small groups using the four-box matrix to develop original stories from pictures or objects of various kinds. You could ask the students to create a story around one of the basic plots that they know.

For example, you might say,

'As a class, let's try making up a tragedy about these boots'.

The storyteller could easily sell the idea that the boots were far too expensive for Henry.

'How did he get them?'

now becomes a key question. Be aware that pupils instinctively problem solve for the quick answers, such as

'He won them' or
'He was given them'.

These can then be reflected upon as a group during this shared experience.

'But is that the most interesting answer for the story?'

you might ask. As soon as Henry has to take dramatic action to obtain these boots, the story starts to get juicy. The fact that he got them but never wore them lends itself well to tragedy. Perhaps he never wore them because he ended up in prison or the boots brought him bad luck. That's the joy of inventing. The storyteller decides. You can create a story from any of the seven plots. Just try. The storyteller's task is simply to make their oral story believable and gripping, which brings its own reward.

Conclusion

Story invention involves generating a sequence of questions, reflecting on potential answers and selecting the best ones for the story. The plot matrix, basic plots, stock characters and standard questions can all be used to help guide and support this process for the students. Your job as teacher is to model their use until the class has got the hang of it. Ultimately these elements will become part of the storymaking toolkit of the students, who will use them naturally when making up stories. Some students make up great stories if they are given lots of freedom and few guidelines. Others need the support of such guidelines to get started with their own ideas.

Almost anything can be used as a stimulus for beginning a story. In this chapter we have used plots, characters, objects and pictures, but you can also use all sorts of stimuli in exactly the same way, including:

➤ paintings

➤ sounds

➤ music

➤ smells

➤ memories

➤ feelings

➤ a word, phrase or quote

In fact pretty much anything that can be experienced by the senses can be used as a stimulus, because that is exactly how our minds work. We experience something and it triggers mental responses. Try to identify stimuli that will excite your class and build on their interests.

Shared writing

Turning oral into written stories

We have described ways of learning, creating and retelling stories using memory, voice and body. Now we will demonstrate how to turn these spoken stories into written ones using shared writing. The class is shown how to write a story using their own ideas before being invited to try for themselves. Shared writing has proved hugely popular in many Storytelling Schools as a way of raising writing standards, as it directly involves teaching students how to craft writing to an appropriate level.

After explaining the basic method, we will describe some variations including shared editing, unilateral demonstration, teaching explicit language features and adaptations for Key Stage 1.

Key principles

In Storytelling Schools, students generally learn to tell and develop a story before they start to write it down. Having mapped, stepped, spoken and deepened a story, they should have plenty of ideas to put on paper. The teacher can then create a written text in front of the class to show them how to write down a story or story section. This shared writing process also allows the teacher to demonstrate writing with a particular aim; rewriting and editing; and how to use explicit language features. In each case, after the shared writing, the students can have a go at writing themselves. The basics of shared writing are summarised in the panel on the right.

Step 1. Choose the story

Decide on the story or story section that is to be used. Students will already have learned and developed the story for oral telling.

Step 2. Define the learning focus

Decide if you want to focus on any learning goals for writing. These might relate to the overall text quality (spooky atmosphere or exciting action) or might also be about modelling a particular language feature (connectives, adverbs, traditional story starters).

Step 3. Draft sample text

Before starting the shared writing session in class, draft a guide text for yourself with the features that you want to teach. This gives you ideas to work with when you demonstrate to the class. Use it to generate a list of questions to ask your class.

Step 4. Create text with the class

Using the ideas your students respond with, draft a text on the board with the class, being explicit about why you have chosen certain ideas and rejected others, or find ways for the class to decide. When the text is drafted, go through again taking suggestions for improvement (shared editing).

Step 5. Independent or guided writing

After the shared text has been generated, students can try independent writing or guided writing in groups, trying to put in practice the things that have been focused upon.

When a story is told orally, the storyteller communicates with the body and voice as well as with words. In writing, there are only the words on the page, so language may need to be used differently to create an engaging text. The shared writing process enables this retelling, teaching the use of literary language, rather than simply transcribing the oral version word for word.

Some students will imitate what they have seen in the shared writing, while more able students may use it as a basis for innovation and invention. The process models the learning triad – **generate, reflect, select** – which has been discussed in previous chapters.

These shared writing methods are only one element in the teaching of writing. For more details on ways of teaching that fit with the Storytelling School model we recommend Pie Corbett's *How to Teach Story Writing KS1, How to Teach Fiction Writing KS2* and *Writing Models* (Fulton Publishers).

General principles of shared writing

Shared writing is a dynamic, interactive form of joint composition. To the students, it should feel as if they are collectively composing and refining a story, with a strong sense of 'making one up together'. However, the teacher is constantly focusing the students' attention onto key aspects, challenging ideas and encouraging the class to create a particular writing objective. At times, the teacher will 'talk aloud like a writer,' explaining clearly the thought processes of a writer whilst generating ideas and selecting which words work best. Shared writing should excite the imagination and awaken the writer in every child. Here are some key principles:

1. Tell and deepen first

Take the students through the stages of storytelling and deepening. This wakes up the story in the student's imagination, stimulates ideas to draw on and adds a sense of playfulness, pleasure and enthusiasm that can be carried through into writing. Students must be able

> ## Sample writing objectives
>
> ➤ Establish character
> ➤ Establish place
> ➤ Describe problem/dilemma and its importance
> ➤ Describe obstacles and their difficulty
> ➤ Describe setbacks and plot twists and turns
> ➤ Describe solution in interesting or surprising way
> ➤ Create a particular mood (tension, excitement, happiness, fear, boredom)
> ➤ Clarity (of action or description)
> ➤ Consistency (does it all make sense?)
> ➤ 'Show don't tell'
> ➤ Multi-sensory description

to tell the story confidently before attempting to write it. The oral rehearsal is invaluable as it frees up students' cognitive abilities when they come to write and allows them to focus on language selection, sentence structure, handwriting, phonics and spelling, rather than on story ideas. Indeed, the younger students and less confident writers should not move into writing unless they can tell their tale.

2. Choose a section of the story

Usually you will want your students to end up writing the whole of the story that they have learned or developed, as this tends to be more satisfying than piecemeal writing. However, in any individual shared writing session, you will normally work on a particular section or paragraph. Sometimes the teacher will move sequentially through the whole story step-by-step, with a shared writing session for each section, perhaps spread over a week or more. Sometimes only selected sections will be taught to practise a particular aspect of writing before letting the students draft the whole thing.

It is usually a good idea to remind the class of the whole story before focusing on a certain section. You can do this with your story map (p. 15), story stepping (p. 16) or by drawing some kind of 'boxing up' diagram that clearly shows the story pattern. Story boards and 'mountains' can also be used.

3. Make the purpose clear

Always focus on the main purpose and effect that you wish to create (developing character and place, establishing a given mood, narrative tension, clarity of descriptions and so on) rather than a specific language goal (such as adverbs, adjectives and connectives). As a teacher you can demonstrate how to achieve effective writing, including use of particular types of words, but the big picture is always about how to create an impact on the reader. Lose that and writing easily becomes mechanical and boring. Being clear about your learning purpose (e.g. creating suspense) is key to the success of your shared writing session. If you do this well, your students will learn how to establish their goals when they write independently.

Thinking like a writer means considering what needs to be conveyed to make the story work. The box on page 78 summarises some common writing purposes. Some are derived from the plot matrix (p. 58) and relate to basic elements of plot. Others are concerned with mood, description, clarity and consistency. The use of multi-sensory descriptions and the core principle of 'show don't tell' are also invaluable techniques to teach to students.

You may have in mind a particular language feature that you want to teach, such as adverb starters, using adjectives and so on. However, remember that the purpose of the writing is to create an effect, such as suspense, and the word choices will help to create that impact. Just using lots of adjectives and adverbs does not make good writing! Focus on creating a good story first of all. The important thing is to get ideas to flow enthusiastically. Some teachers prefer to say, for example, 'Today we are focusing on selecting adjectives', or, 'Let's practise new ways of starting a sentence' and so on. Once the paragraph has been generated, it is much easier to identify words in grammatical terms because the examples and their meaning are understood from the context of the narrative.

What is 'show don't tell'?

This is simply the difference between telling the reader what to think or feel and allowing them to experience that for themselves.

A writer might say, 'The castle was frightening.' Whilst this tells the reader to be scared, the reader would not feel afraid at all. However, if the writer puts the main character in the castle and describes the darkness effectively, then as the reader reads, it is more likely that they imaginatively enter the scene and begin to actually feel afraid. It is the concrete description and action, coupled with the character's reactions, that work on the reader. It is the difference between 'John was cross' and 'John glared as he stormed across the room, his fists clenched.'

4. Make a guide text

In most cases you should write your own 'aspirational' text before starting the session. It is normally above the language level of the top end of the class and will provide a guide for you during shared writing. This text will help you to list prompt questions to ask your class and provide suggestions of words and sentences to add into the mix if needed. It is an invaluable way of keeping your bearings and ensuring that you model your intended learning objectives during the session.

As a teacher you need to be able to draft your own guide text, and work with the questions and answers that arise from that process, in order to develop a suitable text with your class in what is always a fluid and 'live' environment. Most teachers find that, with a bit of practice, this becomes second nature.

5. Involvement in choosing

Students can be given practice in reflecting and selecting by being asked to choose their favourite sentences or words for inclusion in the group text. If, at the point when the sentence is first read out aloud, the class likes a particular word or phrase, it can be repeated out loud, perhaps with a gesture. This helps students to remember the words, makes the whole process more fun, and helps them identify which ideas they will vote for later.

You, as teacher, can choose ideas for including in the shared writing text, modelling a rationale as to why you liked it, even if it's only to say, 'It just felt right'. Other methods can include group or class votes or appointing a pair of editors for each choice, explaining why if possible. With your support, two or three of the ideas could be skilfully combined, adding a sense of inclusion, excitement and drama to the event.

You may want to remind students that they can still use ideas that were not chosen for the class text when they do their own writing. They may want to record these ideas on whiteboards or in their writing journals to use later.

6. Make it playful

Shared writing provides the chance to play with written words. If a story has been told and deepened already, students will already have experienced and used elevated language. These ideas, literary phrases and power words will be up on lists visible on the classroom working wall and can be referred to when students turn to writing. Now, your students can play around with writing them down. Small wipe-boards are invaluable because they enable students, either as individuals or in pairs, to think of words and sentences and write them before sharing and celebrating them with the group. Notebooks (writing journals) for

drafting are also handy because the ideas each student has in the session can be recorded and then used in independent writing. However ideas are recorded, they need to be shared, as far as possible, in a way that is a pleasure.

7. Make it participative

Find ways to get your class involved in creating and sketching out their ideas for words and sentences as often as possible. This will engage students and allow them to rehearse the key skills – **generate, reflect, and select** – within the support of the whole group before trying them out alone. Often this means using talking partners and paired work at each stage of the writing process to allow students to create and share their ideas together. They can then continue with a process of reflection, choosing which idea works best and keeps a sense of engagement and interest for the reader. Making reference to the invisible presence of the reader is important because it shapes the questions we ask of ourselves to create the text and the context for the writing.

8. Make it snappy

Make the response tasks fast to keep the creative energy high and reduce task wandering. For example – you might give groups 30 seconds to write several words or 60 seconds to write a sentence.

9. Independent writing

Once the shared writing class has been completed you can ask the students to have a go themselves, either on their own or in smaller, guided writing groups. Some students may benefit from prompts and worksheets to scaffold their work, but at the independent stage many can be encouraged to write freely, drafting and editing in the way they have been shown. Only by doing all this themselves will they learn to become confident writers.

Three ways to demonstrate writing

Writing is all about creating ideas for a text, generating an initial text, and then improving it. Students need to learn all three of these skills in order to be able to write well independently and the teacher needs to find engaging and effective ways of modelling these skills with the class.

Here we will describe three kinds of modelling: shared writing, shared editing and unilateral demonstrations. All three can be used at different times with your class and in many permutations.

In **shared writing**, new texts are created with the class. Students who have already learned and developed a story and have lots of ideas about it now contribute to creating a written version. In this way, they practise transforming their oral story ideas into written text.

In **shared editing**, the class sees a text and then works with the teacher to improve it. In this way, the students learn how to reflect on and improve their own texts once they have been generated.

A third activity, recommended by us only for quick and occasional use, is **unilateral demonstration**, where teachers demonstrate writing a story to the class, with a running commentary on why certain words and phrases are chosen. Some teachers use this – more often in smaller guided writing groups – to illustrate particular points about writing.

We will now summarise four approaches to shared writing, two types of shared editing and one example of unilateral demonstration. We want to emphasise that while editing is obviously important, we think that shared writing is crucial if a student is to become an independent writer: the first step for the writer is to be able to create a fresh text. Without this, there is nothing much to edit later. If only shared editing is taught, many students will struggle to create their initial narratives.

Shared writing

1. Word for word creation of a new text

Here, no initial text is shown to the class. The teacher asks questions of the class, who respond with suggestions for single key words, e.g. 'What kind of a day was it?', 'What would be a great word to describe the path?', and so on. Then the teacher, using one of a variety of methods of selection, chooses a word and adds it to an emerging text. With this type of shared writing, the teacher leads the creation of sentences. The prompt questions can be derived from the aspirational text and all suggestions offered by the pupils can be charted for future use. The focus is on word selection.

2. Sentence by sentence creation of a text

Here, the focus is on the students contributing sentences – either orally or by using mini white boards. There may be some discussion about the individual selection of words, but the focus moves on to the flow of sentences or clauses. Teachers may choose the one to be adopted or leave that to the class in some way, but the sentences themselves are as written by their authors.

3. New innovated text based on known text format

A model text is shown to the class and used as an explicit guide to creating a new innovated text: for example, the story might be reset in a new place with new characters. The structure of the text is retained but the content is changed and improved. This is what Pie Corbett has called 'hugging the text' because you really get to know the guide text as you write the new one.

4. Shared creative writing and editing combined

This method brings together shared writing and editing, modelling three stages of text refinement: first choose the sentences, then improve them and finally sort the spelling, punctuation and grammar.

Tips for shared writing

✓ Ideally, write on a flipchart so that you do not have your back to the class and you are writing on paper, or use a word processor and use 'track changes' to show editing.

✓ Use a colour, such as red, to make key features stand out.

✓ Say sentences aloud so that everyone can 'listen' to hear whether they work.

✓ Keep re-reading to check for any places where the writing might be improved, for inaccuracies, but also to maintain flow.

✓ Challenge students to encourage them to generate lots of ideas.

✓ Help them to reflect and then choose.

✓ Always bear the reader in mind.

✓ Encourage students to refer to quality books they have read, class readers and model texts.

Shared editing

1. Word by word editing a known text

Here the class is shown a draft text at the beginning of the session and invited to suggest ways of improving it. The teacher will usually ask key questions, have pairs create written suggestions and then either choose one, or get the class to choose one, to add to the edit. Some teachers like to use 'Track Changes' found under the 'Review' menu in Word and write the text up using the computer. This allows pupils to see the changes and the original text. Others like to edit a flipchart text, modelling the editing that happens when writing in a notebook. The focus is on word selection.

2. Sentence by sentence rewriting from a known text

With this method, the class is shown a text that is then rewritten sentence by sentence using suggestions for whole sentences from the students. The general structure given by the shown text is retained in the new draft but the focus is on sentence construction and variation.

Unilateral demonstration modelling

The teacher demonstrates writing text on the board, in front of the class, while giving a running commentary of intention: what is she thinking? Why has she chosen certain words and phrases? How does this link with whatever learning objectives are being demonstrated? This method should be used rarely and for short periods only as the audience is basically passive and may easily get distracted. However, it can be very powerful to think aloud, like a writer.

Examples of shared writing sessions

The rest of this chapter provides some more detailed illustrations of shared writing sessions using the various techniques above. To do this we will start with *Little Red Riding Hood*, using a section of the story where she is walking from her cottage towards the woods. Our writing aim will be to create suspense. Here is our guide text:

Reluctantly, Little Red Riding Hood followed the muddy track from her house towards the dark brooding woods, grumbling to herself as she walked. Stopping and staring at the wall of green in front of her, she remembered the stories her Gran had told her about the dangers of the forest and wondered what was inside. Was that a howl she heard inside the forest, or just the wind in the trees? A flash of grey appeared from behind a tree, just for a moment, and then it was gone. 'Wolves!' she trembled.

Inside the forest canopy it was cold and dark. Shivering, she pulled her thick cloak tight around her shoulders with the hood up over her head. 'This is scary,' she thought. Cautiously, she tiptoed along the path, avoiding any leaf or twig, anxious to be as silent as possible, just in case. Every time she heard a rustle or a snap she'd stop and wait – her heart pounding in her ears – as she listened for any clue for what might be out there away from the path.

The path curved around the base of an ancient oak, trunk as thick as a barrel and as tall as a ship's mast. There was a smell coming from somewhere – 'like a dog', she thought. Suddenly, out of nowhere, a tall dark shape blocked the path, towering above her. It was a wolf, as big as a small horse, its muscles tense and ready to pounce. Fear froze her to the spot as she stared at its lolling tongue and yellow teeth. 'I'm dead!' she thought, and began to cry.

Shared writing example 1:
Word by word creation of a new text

Imagine that the students have been retelling the story of *Little Red Riding Hood*. Let's say that you will work with the first paragraph of the aspirational text, with the aim of creating tension. Use your text to think of a series of questions to ask your class to generate ideas. The table below shows one way of doing this.

Text	Questions for class
Reluctantly, LRRH followed the muddy track from her house towards the dark brooding woods, grumbling to herself as she walked.	1. How is she feeling? Use a sentence opener to describe this (-ed-ing-ly?) 2. What is she doing that tells us she is angry? 3. Let's say she's going along the path to the woods – what words can we use to describe the path? 4. What words can make the woods seem scary?
Stopping and staring at the wall of green in front of her, she wondered what was inside, remembering stories her gran had told her about the dangers of the forest.	5. Now she stops and stares at the wood and starts to feel frightened. What might she be thinking about at that moment that would scare her?
Was that a howl she heard inside the forest, or just the wind in the trees? A flash of grey appeared from behind a tree, just for a moment, then it was gone. 'Wolves!' she thought and trembled.	6. Now she sees and hears something that makes her frightened. What does she see and hear? 7. What does she do that shows us she is frightened?

Now with your prompts to hand, work through, question by question, getting pairs to scribe their suggestions. After choosing a favourite suggestion or suggestions, you can weave them into a sentence for the class to see. Write your prompts on the wall so that they can be referred to later. By sharing your prompt questions each time, you will show that many of them come round again and again, and are generic. In this way, you will explicitly illustrate how to 'think like

a writer'. If your students have a writing journal or a place to record ideas, these questions could be stored there. Focus on selecting the right word. This is the simplest form of innovation.

A new sentence might look like this:

Nervously, Little Red Riding Hood edged along the stony track from her home towards the vast expanse of deep dark forest.

Shared writing example 2: Sentence by sentence creation of a new text

This is based on the same principle as the previous example. Your guide text is still hidden from the class. This time they are expected to generate whole sentences. You need to adjust your prompts, using them to go through the text sentence by sentence. Again either the teacher or students can choose favourite sentences for inclusion in the shared text, while other ideas can be retained by students or charted up on the classroom wall for future use. You might chart up any other good sentences or words for future use. If your students keep a record of their own sentences they can use them when they write independently. Here's an example of sentence level prompts for the guide text:

Original text	Questions for class
Reluctantly, Little Red Riding Hood followed the muddy track from her house towards the dark brooding woods, grumbling to herself as she walked.	Let's start with a sentence that shows how Little Red Riding Hood is feeling as she walks towards the woods. What are the things she sees as she walks? Put this into a sentence.
Stopping and staring at the wall of green in front of her, she wondered what was inside, remembering stories her gran had told her about the dangers of the forest.	As she stares at the wood, how does she feel? How can you show this? Put this into a sentence.
Was that a howl she heard inside the forest, or just the wind in the trees? A flash of grey appeared from behind a tree, just for a moment, then it was gone. 'Wolves!' she thought and trembled.	Now she sees and hears something that makes her even more scared. What does she see and hear and how can we see that she is scared?

Again you can leave the prompts up when the students write independently, or create a worksheet guide if needed, like this:

Questions for class	
How is she feeling? What does she see?	
She's frightened. What is she thinking about?	
What does she see and hear that makes her scared? How can we see that she is scared?	

A new paragraph might look like this:

Sulkily, Little Red Riding Hood slouched along the track, dragging her heels. She stared at the towering wall of green and her heart skipped a beat. There was a flash of grey from inside the canopy. 'What was that?' she thought.

Shared writing example 3:
Creation of new innovated text based on known text

In this example, we create an *innovated* text retelling a known story with a new setting or character. With this method, the class is shown the original text and then has to come up with ideas for an innovated version. In this way, they recycle the language patterns in the original.

Let's say that the class has already learned *Little Red Riding Hood*, and they are going to write their own versions with new characters and settings. The story could be set in a city, where a boy called Red has to walk across a park to play

in a football match. We could show the class an original text and work from it to create a new one, sentence by sentence. This is the process sometimes described as 'hugging'.

The method used is basically the same as in Example 2, except that now the class can see the original sentence and can look for ways to adapt it to the innovated story. This gives them a structure to base their new ideas on. The table below illustrates the kinds of prompt questions you might use to generate suggested sentences.

Original text	*Prompts and examples of innovated sentences*
Reluctantly, LRRH followed the muddy track from her house towards the dark brooding woods, grumbling to herself as she walked.	Red is going to walk out of his house down the road towards the park. Write a sentence to describe the journey and how Red is feeling as he walks. e.g. Cautiously, Red walked along the cracked pavement away from the flats towards the looming gates of the park, muttering to himself.
Stopping and staring at the wall of green in front of her, she wondered what was inside, remembering stories her Gran had told her about the dangers of the forest.	Now Red is going to stare in through the gates. We need to know what he sees, feels and thinks at that moment. e. g. He stared through the iron bars at a wide expanse of grass inside, with a dense cluster of trees at its centre. Remembering the stories his friends had told him about gangs in the park, he shivered..
Was that a howl she heard inside the forest, or just the wind in the trees? A flash of grey appeared from behind a tree, just for a moment, then it was gone. 'Wolves!' she thought and trembled.	Now let him see or hear something to make him even more scared and build up the suspense. e.g. Just then, he heard a voice coming from the cluster of trees and caught a glimpse of a shape moving in the shadows. 'There's someone in there!' he thought, and trembled.

Shared writing example 4:
Shared creative writing and shared editing combined

With this method we move through three stages with the text, all based on the suggestions of the class, with teachers adding in ideas if needed. These stages can be spread over a number of sessions.

Stage 1

The class generates sentences based around prompts from the teacher (see Shared Writing example), until a paragraph of text is created.

Stage 2

The first draft text is edited and improved using suggestions from the class (See Shared Writing examples 1 and 2, pp. 84 and 85). To improve the quality of the writing, the three focusing questions here are always the same, 'What can I change? What can I add? What can I take away?'

Stage 3

The class suggests changes in spelling, punctuation and grammar to complete the text. In this way, the class is led through creation and refinement of the text.

The seven-step method

Here is a detailed example using an excerpt from *Baba Yaga's Black Geese*, available on the Story Museum website:
www.storymuseum.org.uk/1001stories

Using a section of the *Baba Yaga* story, we are going to create a multi-sensory piece of writing. There are seven steps to this process: choosing the story, defining the learning focus, drafting sample text, creating text with the class, first shared editing, second shared editing, and independent or guided writing.

Step 1: Choose the story or story section

For this example, we will focus on the moment when Olga enters the witch's hut.

Step 2: Define the learning focus

We will aim to write a piece that evokes a sense of place and a feeling of fear, using multi-sensory description.

Step 3: Draft sample text

Before you draft your sample text, you and your class will have explored some of the deepening activities that directly support your objectives in the writing. During these activities you will have brainstormed descriptive words for the various senses that might be applied to the witch's hut, such as 'What does Olga see? Smell? Hear? Feel and think?' These words can be recorded on a large sheet, or on whiteboards by individuals or pairs, and might look something like this:

Hear	Smell
Strange scuttling, hissings, bubbling and snorting sounds	Burning wood and foul aromas – rotting meat – mould
See	**Feel/Think**
The darkness itself – as black as ... (explore similes). Rocking chair, cauldron, witch's broom/spell book	Cold/scared/sweat pouring from her brow/What am I doing here?/ What's that smell?/ I should have listened to my mum

Using the resulting word list you might draft a guide/aspirational text like the one below for a Year 4/5 class. It should be just above the current level of the top of the class.

With sweat pouring from her brow, Olga slowly pushed open the door. 'What's that smell?' she gasped, quickly pinching her nose, 'It's worse than the stench of rotting meat.' Stepping cautiously into the hut was like walking into a shadow – a thing so dark there was nothing but black. 'What am I doing here?' Olga trembled. She felt something brush against her foot. 'Was that a cat?'

A long, groaning creak drew Olga's eyes deeper into the darkness until they fell on the outline of a stooped, twisted figure, slowly prising itself away from a charred and splintered rocking chair by the fire. 'Run!' screamed a voice in Olga's head. She tried to turn, to run, to move. But she couldn't. She was stone: cold and terrified.

Step 4: Create text with the class

First explain the learning goals, and then get the class to brainstorm ideas for the various senses, just as you did yourself. Now start to ask questions based around your sample text. This time you might work with whiteboards to give students practice at writing and rewriting.

Your sample text gives a draft sequence of events to refer to and use if you get stuck. You could start by saying: 'Write one short opening sentence that shows the reader how Olga is feeling as she opens the door.' Alternatively, you might allow pupils to choose their own way into the paragraph. Give them 90 seconds to draft a sentence, then hear a few and choose your favourite, giving a reason for your choice if possible.

Once the class has got the hang of this idea, you can cast two students in the role of 'publishers', giving them the job of choosing their favourite sentence and explaining why if they can. Always remember, however, that what we are trying to develop is a sense of writer's intuition. Sometimes the explanation can be as simple as 'It just felt right'. Make sure you keep rotating the role of publishers.

Proceed like this, sentence by sentence, until you have generated a paragraph of shared writing on the board. When writing this up some teachers like to use the computer with 'track changes' so that, during the editing stage, the class can always see the original draft and how it has developed.

At this point you can, depending on the time available, either move straight onto the next step or give your students an opportunity to write their own first draft, leaving an empty line for their edits between each line of written text in their books.

Step 5: First shared edit

Let's say the shared writing produced this text:

Olga pushed the door open with a trembling hand and stepped into the hut. The putrid smell of rotting meat almost made her gag. 'What am I doing here?' she shivered. Suddenly, she felt something brush against her foot. "Rats!" she squealed. Her eyes shot to the ground but whatever it was had gone, vanishing into the dark recesses of the room, before she could truly see what it had been.

The aim of the first edit is to improve the overall language quality. If your main objective was a particular point of grammar e.g. the use of adjectives or extending sentences through the use of parenthesis, you may want to shift your focus to this now. However, a good way to approach a generic first edit for improving the writing quality can be to always ask the same

Chapter 8   Shared writing

three questions of each sentence as you have done using the other editing methods:

'What can we change? What can we add? What can we take away?'

Take the first sentence from the board and ask students to draft an improved version. Ask the class the three generic questions: what to add, delete and change? You might also encourage them to focus on a writer's objective, for example, to make clearer how Olga steps into the room, or describe the door a little, or whatever comes to mind.

Give the students 90 seconds to talk in pairs and make suggestions for editing that first sentence. Again, before hearing these ideas, say,

'I want all of you to decide which of these ideas you like best'.

As a teacher, you can decide which changes to accept, or give the choice over to a group of students.

So, the first sentence might evolve to this:

Olga pushed the door open with a trembling hand and stepped cautiously into the hut.

With a bit more work, perhaps focusing on extending the sentence to drop in a subordinate clause, the sentence might look like this:

Olga, sweat pouring from her brow, pushed the door open with a trembling hand and slipped slowly and cautiously into the witch's hut.

To help you to keep focused while working on this first edit, refer back to the original objectives, which might relate to tension, a sense of place and so on. Remember that you can always work on 'show don't tell' ideas at this stage too.

Very able writers often produce fancy sentences using a whole string of adjectives during the first draft. Checking sentences against the prompt 'What can we delete or take out?' reveals the effectiveness of using fewer, but more powerful, adjectives and adverbs to achieve our aims. In this way, you can work, sentence by sentence, through the shared writing, always reading from the top before editing the next sentence.

Step 6: Second shared edit (grammar and punctuation)

Once the second draft is complete, you can recheck the draft for punctuation, spelling and grammar. You might go through the current text sentence by sentence, asking students to spot things that need changing. You might try adding a few errors to make the experience interesting.

Step 7: Independent and guided writing

Now the students can go through the same process with their own text, producing a first draft, then doing a first edit for content and a second edit for grammar, spelling and punctuation. Those who need support can be coached through in a guided writing group.

This model for shared writing also works in sessions where pupils have created their own stories, for a wide range of settings and contexts. You can use the shared sessions to remind them of things to look at in their texts, and how to review learning goals and sequence their edits, before embarking on their own stories.

There is very little difference between shared writing sessions with Year 1 and Year 6 in the progression of these activities and the basic principles outlined. The complexity of the story and the language features you focus on are what will vary.

Examples of shared editing

In shared editing, the class is shown a text in need of improvement and then helps improve it by making and selecting suggestions to add, delete and change. Here we give two examples: the first is word-for-word editing and the second sentence-by-sentence. Offering the class a very poor initial text can create enthusiasm and focus for improvement.

Shared editing example 1: Word-for-word editing of a known text

Here you would start off with a weak text that you have prepared, to provide a basis for a particular learning focus. You don't put the good stuff in the initial text: that's the job of your class.

You might show the first paragraph like this. Numbers show the place to which the question applies.

(1) Little Red Riding Hood (2) followed the track from her house to the (3) woods. She was angry with her mum. She looked at the woods and felt scared in case there was a wolf inside. She remembered stories her gran had told her about wolves. Just then she saw a movement inside and thought, 'It's a wolf!'

Then say:

'Now we're going to edit this to see which bits we can improve whether adding, deleting or changing.'

Q1. 'Let's think of a sentence starter that tells us how LRRH is feeling right now. Talk to your partner and write your idea on a whiteboard. It could be an -ing, -ed or -ly word'.

Your students show their ideas on their whiteboards. You celebrate ideas by repeating them out loud, model your reflection and then you choose e.g. 'Okay, I choose "cautiously".' You then make the edit.

Q2 'Instead of "followed", what word could we use to show how she was feeling?'

Pairs then write their word and again you choose. (For example, choose 'slunk'.)

Q3 'How can we add describing words to make the woods seem scary to her?'

Again students write down their ideas, show you and you choose, for example, 'deep, dark'.

Now our sentence is:

Cautiously, LRRH slunk along the track from her house to the deep dark woods.

Here's our next sentence:

She was angry with her mum.

'What could we add here so we know that she is angry by what she does. What would we see or hear that would tell us that?'

Appreciate, reflect out loud and choose, for example, 'grumbled' and 'scowled'.

She grumbled to herself as she walked, with a fixed scowl on her face.

And so on. At the end of the process, discuss the learning points and then let your students have a go at doing their own editing.

Shared editing example 2: Sentence-by-sentence rewriting of a given text

This is basically the same as example 1 except that instead of taking ideas for individual words and phrases to add, delete or subtract from each sentence, you ask the class to rewrite the whole sentence in order to make it even better.

Let's say we are working with the same given text as in example 1. The class would then see, on the board:

Little Red Riding Hood followed the track from her house to the woods. She was angry with her mum. She looked at the woods and felt scared in case there was a wolf inside. She remembered stories her gran had told her about wolves. Just then she saw a movement inside and thought, 'It's a wolf!'

You might read the text through and then say:

'The first sentence describes what LRRH is doing as she walks towards the woods. Let's think of sentences that describe how she walks and where she walks more clearly.'

Then pairs can write their sentences on a whiteboard before one is chosen for the class text. You can also get your students to talk about the function of each sentence before drafting their own version.

Example of unilateral demonstration

This is a way of demonstrating writing to a class with no or little student input. You can use it to quickly illustrate a practical point about writing. With this method the teacher simply writes in front of the class while explaining to them what she is thinking about as she writes.

Here's an example of such a monologue using *Little Red Riding Hood*. What is written on the board is shown in bold. As well as creating tension, the teacher is showing varied sentence starters (-ed, -ing, -ly) and the writer's principle of 'show don't tell'. The teacher could say:

'I'm wondering how to start this section, maybe with something that tells us how Little Red Riding Hood is feeling. What could that be – slowly? nervously? reluctantly? I'll go with reluctantly. It's good to use one of the words ending in -ed, -ing -ly, as a start to a sentence.'

So, choose 'reluctantly'.

'Now let's describe something about the walk so our reader can see it. She's walking along the path towards the wood so let's just say that, let's make it muddy so it's not too welcoming.'

Reluctantly LRRH followed the muddy track from her house towards the woods.

'Now I want to add suspense. How can we describe the woods to make them scarier? I'll go with dark, brooding.'

So the story becomes:

Reluctantly LRRH followed the muddy track from her house towards the dark, brooding woods.

'Now I want something about how she is feeling. Let's use the principle of 'show don't tell' here for writing – she's feeling a bit annoyed with her mum – let's describe something she does that tells us that.'

Reluctantly, LRRH followed the muddy track from her house towards the dark, brooding woods, grumbling to herself as she walked.

Then you can ask them to have a go themselves, or show another sentence in the same way, which builds more tension.

Example of teaching specific language features

If you want to teach a particular language feature, you can devise a sample text to illustrate its use, then create a shared writing text with the class that includes it, and ask pupils to write their own text using the same feature. For example, the text on page 92 could be used to reinforce the use of time connectives. The overall learning focus might be to have a clear sense of the passing of time in the story. You can illustrate how to do this with 'when', 'until' and 'after'.

Let's say we are going to practise adding the words 'until', 'because', 'when', 'after', and 'that'.

You might draft the following sample text, explain to the class that they will be practising using those words, and then create a shared text using questions and answers. The process would otherwise be the same as in the previous examples.

When Olga realised that the geese had taken her brother, she was determined to rescue him. She ran and she ran and she ran through the forest until she came to a river. She was wondering what to do next when she heard a voice calling up to her. It was a fish, lying on the bank, gasping for air.

'Help me,' said the fish, 'because if you help me then I will help you.'

She dropped the fish back into the river and waited until it swam up to the surface with a shell in its mouth.

'This will help you if you are in trouble,' it said.

Olga took the shell and the fish disappeared into the water. After that, she came to a squirrel that was caught in a trap.

'Help me,' said the squirrel, 'because if you help me then I will help you.'

Example of adaptations for KS1

Giving choices

For young children it can be useful to give word choices at different parts of the story rather than ask them to make up whole sentences. Here's one way to prepare text using *The Freedom Song* story. You can stop at every bracket and ask the class to choose from one of the options given or make up one of their own.

(Once upon a time, Long ago, Once, not twice, not thrice) there was a hunter who lived in a *(small, tiny, lovely little)* village of *(huts, houses, homes)* in the middle of a *(deep, dark, lovely, beautiful)* forest. One *(sunny, dark, windy)* morning the hunter was walking through the forest past *(trees, bushes, lions, tigers)* when he came to a tree. Something moved in the tree, so he looked up and saw a *(lovely, wonderful, amazing, strange, and weird)* bird perched on a branch. He thought *(wow what a lovely bird/how beautiful/what cool colours)* and so decided not to shoot it. Just then the bird started to sing. When the hunter heard the song he felt *(cross, annoyed, confused, angry)*. 'Was the bird making fun of him?' he thought.

Writing from character

Let's say a Year 1 class has learned to tell *Little Red Riding Hood* and now you want them to start writing a text. First it might be helpful to remind the class of the wolf's character by some physicalising exercises. For most students, this process is very powerful and puts the story more securely into the visual part of their 'writer's brain'.

Your sample text might include the phrase:

A big, bad, hairy, scary wolf, with two long pointy ears, two red fiery eyes, sharp claws and teeth dripping with blood!

Before starting shared writing, you might rehearse this chanted description while encouraging the students to copy your actions. To place the physical description of the wolf inside your minds and bodies you might take a wide, menacing stance, draw the two long pointy ears with your hands in the air, point to your fiery eyes, show your claws and your dripping teeth. Invite the students to prowl around the room in wolf character, lurking behind an imaginary tree, pouncing, roaring and brandishing sharp claws. You might ask the students to greet each other using Wolf's growly, gravelly voice or simply replay the sequence of the story where they have to use Wolf's growly, gravelly voice to say, 'All the better to see you with'. In short, having great fun being Wolf while reusing all the vocabulary you want them to use in their writing.

After that you might move on to working with the whiteboards, directing the students to sound out and write 'big', 'bad', 'hairy', 'scary', followed by the next bit and so on. You could play games choosing the most difficult words to sound out, 'fiery eyes and teeth dripping with blood', writing them up on the board and then rubbing a word out so the students have to recall it. You can work, section by section, through the story keeping things playful and engaged.

Thinking like a writer

Shared writing is all about demonstrating the principle of 'thinking like a writer'. This means thinking about the effect you want to have on your reader and the best way to achieve the effect. Throughout the shared writing session we ask this question again and again – what are we trying to achieve and what's the best idea so far to achieve it? To do this we imagine what it would be like to read the text, and what will make that experience better. Setting writers objectives, generating ideas and choosing the best ones: that's thinking like a writer.

Teachers as writers

As teachers, we need to become good enough writers in order to pass on our knowledge to our students. We learn this by teaching it. By writing alongside our pupils, we will become progressively more experienced in the process of writing and the teaching of it. We will then, with some confidence, be able to say, 'Here are some things I know about writing because I write myself.' All of the examples given in this chapter will help you develop this knowledge. You don't have to be a perfect or professional writer. It's just being confident enough to (a) draft your own guide texts and (b) review ideas as they come up from the class and explain what it is about some of the ideas that work well. Most importantly of all – relax and enjoy yourselves!

Chapter 9

Non-fiction: Six types of communication

Introduction

Teaching 'non-fiction' is sometimes understood to be about learning how to write texts of various types. However, in a Storytelling School the spoken elements of 'non-fiction' communication are given great importance. Whether informal conversation skills or formal presentations, these communication skills are essential and important for everyone to learn.

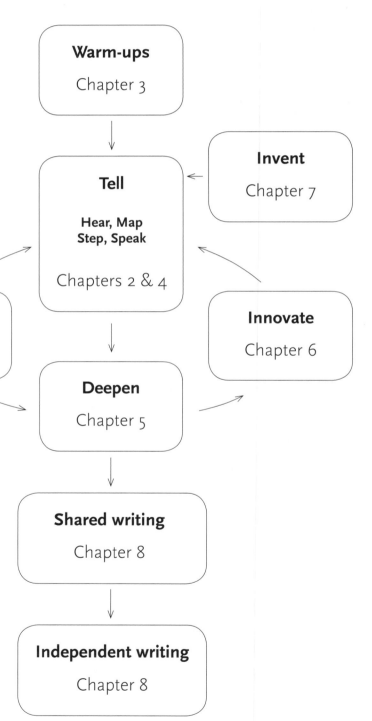

All the principles and methods explained in the previous chapters are applicable to non-fiction too. It's really the same thing: learning to plan, sequence and communicate ideas in various ways by learning to speak them, deepen, innovate and invent through spoken versions and linking those versions into writing.

Here's a reminder of the scheme in the rest of the book which we will apply in this chapter too.

We will focus on the six areas of non-fiction in the current English primary curriculum, although the same principles can be applied to any area of non–fiction presentation and report writing.

Following the same scheme as in the rest of the book, we will discuss the following teaching elements:

➤ Warm it up

➤ Telling it

➤ Deepening it

➤ Innovating the telling

➤ Inventing a new telling

➤ Shared and then independent writing from the imitated, innovated or invented tellings.

The six types of communication we will discuss here are:

1. **Recount**
   (retelling what happened)

2. **Instruction**
   (how to do something)

3. **Persuasion**
   (why you should do something)

4. **Discussion**
   (pros and cons of an issue)

5. **Information**
   (facts about something)

6. **Explanation**
   (how something works or happened, cause and effect)

We are using the phrase 'types of communication' to emphasise that these communication functions may be expressed orally, or in various other ways, not just in writing.

Why do they matter?

Oral competence in these six types of communication is incredibly important in everyday life whether in work, relationships or leisure. They define some of the core, essential communication skills that we all need to be productive, successful and happy. Some homes are rich in these types of conversations, enabling children to master them earlier and more easily. Where these types of conversations are unfamiliar to students, the teacher's job is to provide models and practice for students to catch up during school time. Rehearsing these ideas orally is a fast, natural and effective way to achieve this.

A person who leaves school unable to communicate effectively in these ways is at an enormous disadvantage compared to their more eloquent peers.

Imagine being married to someone who struggles to explain what happened and why, to put a point of view, to give clear instructions, or who has difficulty engaging in thoughtful discussion. How would that impact on the relationship?

Imagine how this might impact on parenting.

In a work context, imagine working in a shop and struggling to explain to customers how something works and how to use it, or to explain to the boss what happened when he was away or to discuss with a colleague what needs doing.

These skills are perhaps among the most essential to equip us for a fulfilling life. They teach us not only ways of communicating but also ways of thinking.

Teaching these functions really matters.

In addition, children are expected to learn the basics of these six types of communication in primary school so that they can develop and use them across the curriculum in secondary school. If they have not mastered the basics in primary then they may well struggle to keep up at secondary school. Mastery of these written forms is crucial for progress in the school education system and beyond into any jobs involving communications.

Similarities to fiction teaching

The methods in this book are about learning to communicate through speaking and writing using warm-ups, storytelling, deepening, innovation, invention and shared writing as a link to independent writing. This sequence is directly applicable to the teaching of these six types of 'non-fiction' communication in more or less the same way. Here are some of the common features:

➤ Both can be understood through role-plays and other warm-up games

➤ Both have a beginning, which sets the scene, a middle where the core content is explored and an ending, which completes the communication in some way

➤ Both can be learned orally and deepened to develop language ideas before linking them to writing

➤ Both can be learned communally (word for word) or independently (improvising language)

➤ Both can be modelled using shared writing

➤ Both have standard patterns similar to the seven basic plots, which can be used to teach basic structures of an oral or written presentation

➤ Both, once learned, can be changed through innovation

➤ Both can be created fresh for a particular purpose (invention)

➤ Both can be explored using fictional or fantasy content

Differences from fiction teaching

In addition there is an important difference between fiction and non-fiction teaching: some kinds of non-fiction tend to use more standard forms of language and structure. Accordingly there can be more value in learning the text or presentation word-for-word so that these language patterns can be thoroughly mastered.

Standard forms

With some kinds of non-fiction texts there are quite precise language conventions and structures that need to be learned, whereas with fiction there is often more flexibility.

I know from my (Chris) own experience how useful these patterns are. For example, when I was about 12 years old I learned the following report pattern for experiments:

➤ Introduction (purpose, background, hypothesis)

➤ Method (what the experimenter did)

➤ Results (what happened)

➤ Conclusion (what we can learn from this)

Since then, whenever I write about any kind of experiment or trial involving observation and reflection, this is my default report structure. I may change it a bit but this is deep in my way of thinking about reports. My PhD has exactly this structure. With fiction the ordering of things is much more flexible.

Likewise I learned at school to write these reports in the past third person tense together with a bunch of phrases and stock sentences like:

➤ The purpose of this experiment was to...

➤ The experiment tested the following hypothesis...

➤ In 2009 Smith and Smith reported that...

> The table below shows the results for...

> This data supports the hypothesis that...

I still use all this language 40 years later: it provides a way of thinking, organising ideas and communicating them effectively. Thank you, science teachers! And the great thing is that this simple scheme is applicable to every kind of experimental investigation. Once you've learned it you can apply it anywhere.

Non-fiction is like that. Learn the basic patterns, practise a bit, and then it's easy to apply them in any context.

Telling the text

Often with non-fiction you may want to teach the class to tell a text word-for-word in order to thoroughly learn the language patterns and structures used. It's like communal telling for fiction stories.

For this you may sometimes want to use a text mapping technique where individual words are mapped and embodied with particular gestures. This accelerates text learning. Such level is rarely needed for fiction where it is usually enough to map and step the overall plot.

Using fantasy and fiction

While the ultimate aim of learning these six types of communication is to be able to apply them to real life subjects, there is a great advantage in learning them first using fantasy topics, because then you can concentrate on teaching the structure and language and just make up the content. Then when students innovate and invent their own stories they can make up their own content without having to worry about facts. Once the class has got the hang of the form then you can apply it to 'factual' topics where the content needs to be researched. Dragons are a very popular starting point.

Using fantasy topics can also provide a useful tool for assessment – it allows the assessment of the language and the structure used without children having to know lots of facts about a topic.

Another option is to use elements from a story that the class already knows so that the content is easily generated. This may be related to a story that has been learned recently by the class. Many Storytelling Schools spend the first three weeks of a half term exploring a fiction story and the second half looking at a related non-fiction function. For example, if the fiction story is *Cinderella* then the class might study discussion texts looking at issues like how should the sisters be punished, or persuasion as the prince tries to persuade Cinderella to marry him.

The structure of this chapter

For the rest of this chapter we will go through the same steps for teaching non-fiction:

➤ warm-ups

➤ imitation (spoken)

➤ innovation (spoken)

➤ invention (spoken)

➤ shared and independent writing linked to the above

We have tried to emphasise the importance of working orally before moving on to the writing. We are not suggesting you always do all these things when teaching non-fiction: mix and match as needed.

These can be used and adapted for all six types of non-fiction communication and any other kind of report format.

Specifically we will cover the following areas:

Areas covered in chapter:

Warm-ups

➤ role-play

➤ read and discuss sample texts

➤ watch, discuss and retell sample presentations

➤ watch, discuss and retell sample clips from fiction videos

➤ create hook for theme of main non-fiction theme

Imitate

➤ learn orally

➤ develop orally

➤ deepen

➤ discuss report structure

➤ create a 'tool kit' of useful language features

Innovate

➤ shared innovation

➤ independent innovation

Invent

➤ shared invention

➤ independent invention

Shared and independent writing

➤ innovation example

➤ invention example

Application across the curriculum

Warm-ups

Role-play games

In a storytelling classroom students can rehearse one or more of the six types of communication every single day using role-play games. These can be quick, simple and fun, building familiarity, confidence, knowledge of language patterns and fluency in their use.

Typically a teacher might:

➤ Demonstrate a role-play scenario to the class

➤ Allow small groups to practise the exercise

➤ Offer opportunities for performance back to the class

The initial brief demonstration allows you to give ideas and model particular language features that others may copy. The small group work allows active engagement with the exercises and feedback plenary allows the class to learn from others and to sometimes enjoy the spotlight of performance. The whole thing might take 10–15 minutes, although there is always the opportunity to spend more time developing the warm-ups into performance and writing if desired.

There is an infinite variety of topics to choose from when designing your warm-ups. Topics may be chosen from:

➤ Personal experience (what happened to me)

➤ Realistic imagined events (i.e. invented but true to normal life)

➤ Fantasy events (invented where anything is possible)

➤ Related to a known fiction story (i.e. happening to a character in a known story)

In all cases the exercise needs to have an explicit character, audience and purpose. It needs to be clear:

➤ who is speaking,

➤ why they are speaking, and

➤ to whom they are speaking.

The main thing then is to choose subjects which will interest and engage your students and about which they have enough knowledge to improvise speech.

For example, let's say that most of your class are really passionate about football. Below are some scenarios for oral exploration of the various types of communication.

Football-related warm-ups for the six functions

Function	Scenario	Character/Setting
Recount	What happened in my last match	Explaining to friend on the phone
Persuasion	Why club X should buy or sell a particular player	TV football talk show
Discussion	Should we have goal line technology?	Expert presentation at football conference
Explanation	How the offside trap works	Coach to players
Information	About premiership footballers	TV documentary, interview
Instructions	Tactics before game	Coach to players

Obviously all of these exercises could sometimes be linked to quick pieces of practice writing if you wish, such as:

➤ newspaper report

➤ letter to a friend

➤ diary entry

➤ handbook entry

You might also fit in here a piece of writing to use for 'cold' assessment to understand the elements which need teaching in the shared writing stage and assess progress later on.

You can also draw on personal material for the role-plays. Below are a few examples. You need to find subjects where everyone in the class can draw on their own experience in some way.

Here are a few more ideas, this time based on more general personal experience:

Personal warm-ups for the six functions

Function	Scenario	Character/Setting
Recount	Something which happened to me last week/year or related to particular stimulus	Explaining to friend on the phone
Persuasion	Persuading a friend to do something (stop smoking, stealing, fighting)	Playground conversation
Discussion	Thinking through the pros and cons of a decision about something (change schools, start karate, learn the guitar)	Discussion with parents, teacher, friends
Explanation	Explain to a friend about how something works (mobile phone, netball match, video game, bicycle)	Explaining to a friend
Information	Talk about something you are interested in (horses, dragons, princesses, pirates)	Talk to a friend or present to a conference
Instructions	Choose something you know how to do: teach it to someone else (read music, play piano, catch a bus to town, win a fight, ride a horse...)	Role-play the lesson

Another option is to choose as context a story which the class already knows and likes, and use that to create a suitable scenario. For example, let's say the class has been working on *The Freedom Song* so they have plenty of information and ideas already. You could suggest one of the following:

➤ Recount: what happened to the hunter or bird retold to mother

➤ Persuasion: hunter persuading a friend not to try and kill freedom birds

➤ Discussion: fishermen discuss pros and cons of opening the box

➤ Explanation: why it is futile to try and kill freedom birds

➤ Instructions: how to cook freedom bird pie

➤ Information: about freedom birds (expert presentation)

It's good to get used to making up your own oral warm-ups so you can adapt to your class's own needs as they develop. You'll find it's easy and quick once you get the hang of it. Let's say you are concentrating on persuasion for a few weeks; you might include the following scenarios:

➤ Persuading a dragon to stop eating children

➤ TV advert persuading people to buy a new kind of hat/shoe/etc.

➤ Talk show role-play where you try to persuade the host that you were right to blow up the school/have a dragon for a pet/ leave school and become a pirate

➤ Little Red Riding Hood tries to persuade the wolf to stop eating people

➤ Jack tries to persuade his mother that it was a good idea to buy the beans

➤ The prince tries to persuade Cinderella to marry him at the ball

➤ The wolf tries to persuade the pig in the brick house to open the door

➤ A child persuading a dalek to stop killing

➤ You persuading a teacher to do more singing/ dancing/football/karate/storytelling

➤ Persuading a bully to stop bullying

➤ A witch persuading a good child to become a witch

➤ Devil persuading a kind child to be cruel

➤ A field persuading a cloud to rain

➤ A tree persuading the sun to shine

You might also brainstorm a list of favourite subjects and then together think of scenarios to include them over the period of study, mixing personal ideas, fiction and fantasy. When ready, let them invent their own scenarios and vote for favourite ones.

Read and discuss sample texts

It's important for children to get used to good quality texts and to understand what is good about them. They have to know what 'good' is in order to be able to aim for it. Having the class read through various texts, discuss what they like about them and have the teacher point out some key features is a good way to do this. This can happen in preparation in the warm-up stage, and also during the process of imitation and invention. It helps students to think like a writer: i.e. what is it for, what works well and what shall I adapt for my own piece of work. The class might sometimes choose a favourite text and then work on it in depth using imitate, innovate and invent. You will find examples of texts in books like Pie Corbett's *Writing Models*. Some teachers have a collection of texts for each type of communication. Others make their own up.

Watch, discuss and retell sample presentations

It's equally important for students to know what a good presentation is like. A great way to do this is to watch short presentation clips, then discuss and perhaps have a go at imitating the presentation style and structure. You can also use clips from talk shows, football commentary, soaps, sports on TV, DJ chat – anything where these types of communication are being used.

Watch, discuss and retell sample clips from fiction videos

Fiction stories are full of moments where a character is communicating using one of the six types of non-fiction communication. You can show them the clip and then role-play that moment.

For example, in *Lord of the Rings* you might use:

Recount: Gandalf explains to Aragorn what happened to him with the fire dragon

Persuasion: Pippin persuades Treebeard to take a different route

Discussion: Gandalf and Elrond discuss what to do with the ring

Explanation: Gandalf explains to Frodo about the history of the ring of power and how it was created

Instructions: Gollum gives himself instructions about how to lead Frodo to the monster spider

Information: Boromir tells Aragorn about Gondor.

Choose a movie you and your class both know and work from there.

Cross-curricular opportunities

In most subjects the six types of communication will come up in class discussion and in presentations of various kinds. You can use these as opportunities to develop your students' communication skills by:

➤ being explicit about what type of communication they are being asked to use

➤ demonstrating modelling of particular patterns and language features

➤ practice time for oral rehearsal in small groups

➤ whole class reflection

'Hook' for theme of main text

This is a way of introducing a main topic or text in a way that gets the students engaged and excited about the theme. Here are a few examples from Storytelling Schools where we have worked, including fantasy topics:

➤ For a text about aliens put a big crate or container and parachute in the playground and announce that it came from outer space. Have a policeman give a talk to the class on the dangers of aliens.

➤ For dragons you could announce that a dragon has been sighted locally and have a visiting professor talk about the sighting.

➤ For pirates you could have a video link with a pirate and interview him with the class.

➤ There might be an object related to the theme that might be shown, explained and researched.

➤ For 'realistic' topics you might collect objects, video clips and information texts and share them in various ways or visit a relevant place to stimulate the imagination.

The main thing is to kick the theme off with something unexpected which stimulates interest and excitement.

Sequencing your non-fiction teaching

After the warm-ups you can follow the same basic teaching sequence as for fiction narratives:

Imitate: first learn to speak the non-fiction idea, either word-for-word or more freely (independent telling where students add their own language ideas)

Innovate: keep the same basic pattern and innovate by changing the content

Invent: change the pattern to suit a new subject and apply across the curriculum as needed

Write: shared and independent writing linked to imitated, innovated or invented tellings.

For the rest of this chapter we will go through one detailed example of a teaching sequence linking to our key story for this book, *The Freedom Bird*. The example will create information pieces with a focus on birds.

Before beginning such a teaching sequence you may have warmed up the topic by role-playing bird experts presenting ideas to the TV, being interviewed about made up birds and brainstorming all the different facts you might want to know about birds.

Imitation

For non-fiction you will often create or find a suitable text to work from orally, which has the language features and patterns in it that you want to teach your class. You can see Pie and Julia's book for detailed examples if you need them (see page 158).

Often teachers start off with fantasy themes in order to teach the structure before applying them to factual subjects. For example, you could make up a text like this about the Jub-Jub bird that could be an entry in the handbook of mythic birds.

The Jub-Jub bird

Did you know that the Jub-Jub bird is the heaviest flying creature in the world?

It can easily be distinguished by its large size and distinctive colour. Mature birds are about the size of a large horse with purple wings and a pink body. Their beaks are long and thin and coloured silver, while their claws are like sharp knives and black. Female Jub-Jub birds smell like custard while males have no smell at all.

Juvenile birds can be identified by their yellow and black wings and their bald featherless heads. They smell of bananas.

Jub-Jub birds are shy and only live far away from human habitation, deep in forests or high up in the mountains. They live underground and dig deep tunnels and caves with their strong sharp claws. Each family has its own cave, and the tunnels all connect up to a huge cave where the birds meet and dance every evening.

In recent years Jub-Jub birds have been hunted close to extinction. In some countries Jub-Jub claws are thought to bring good luck. Many people are willing to pay a high price for a Jub-Jub necklace leading to the killing of birds for their claws. Even though this practice is now illegal it still continues to this day.

If you see Jub-Jub claws for sale, report it immediately to the police and help protect these wonderful birds.

If you have particular language features that you want to teach, then you might make sure they are in the text.

1.1 Learn to tell the story

a. Word-for-word oral imitation

Pie Corbett has come up with a brilliant way to remember texts word-for-word by creating a word and phrase map for the text. It is a bit like a story map but includes individual words and phrases, and so is more detailed.

Using this method, first tell the piece (or a section of it) with the class a few times using a 'word map' to help them remember it and then have them tell from the map a few times. Below is an example of a map for the first paragraph of the Jub-Jub bird text. Once you have demonstrated the method children should be able to make up their own maps, which will help them learn the text more easily.

It is also really important to have physical movements to go with the words to help memory, aid concentration and generally to make it all more fun. If you want to see an example of movements to support telling a non-fiction piece look at the clip called 'stories and non-fiction' on the **storytellingschools.com** website to see how it can be done. There are plenty of other examples on the internet to watch.

Some teachers like to read the text first with the class. This is possible, however we recommend storytelling first and reading and writing later, to fully make use of the oral side of the brain first. This follows the same scheme we used for fiction storytelling.

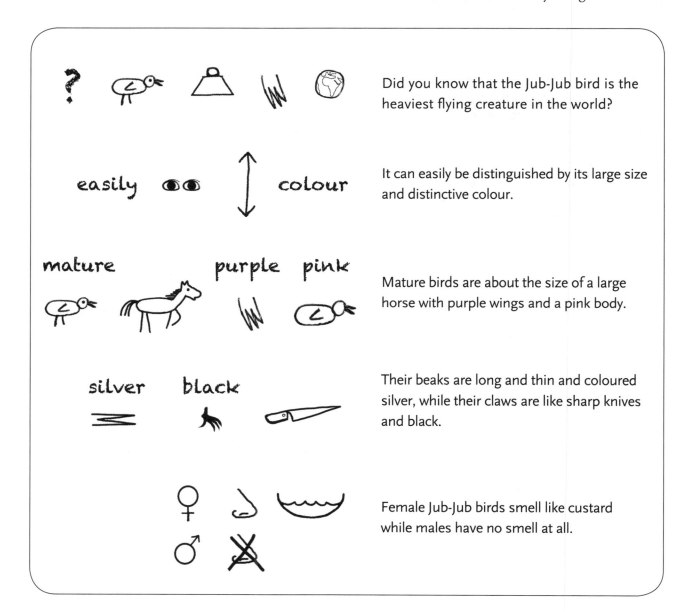

Did you know that the Jub-Jub bird is the heaviest flying creature in the world?

It can easily be distinguished by its large size and distinctive colour.

Mature birds are about the size of a large horse with purple wings and a pink body.

Their beaks are long and thin and coloured silver, while their claws are like sharp knives and black.

Female Jub-Jub birds smell like custard while males have no smell at all.

Chapter 9   Non-fiction: Six types of communication

You might start off by chanting the piece together a few times as a class, then get small groups to practise in various ways (pairs together, story circle, back and forth in pairs and so on) until everyone can perform the text from their 'word map' independently. Some children find it easier to step through each step in the piece once it has been mapped with a physical gesture for each phrase to help remember it. Let your class try that too and see if it works better.

b. Hear, Map, Step, Speak

Alternatively, or afterwards, you may also choose to learn the piece in a more independent way using the HMSS method from Chapter 4. With HMSS the telling is more independent, with the students making up their own language if they want to from the start.

One way to do this is first to map and step the structure. The figure below shows an icon and gesture for the structure of this piece.

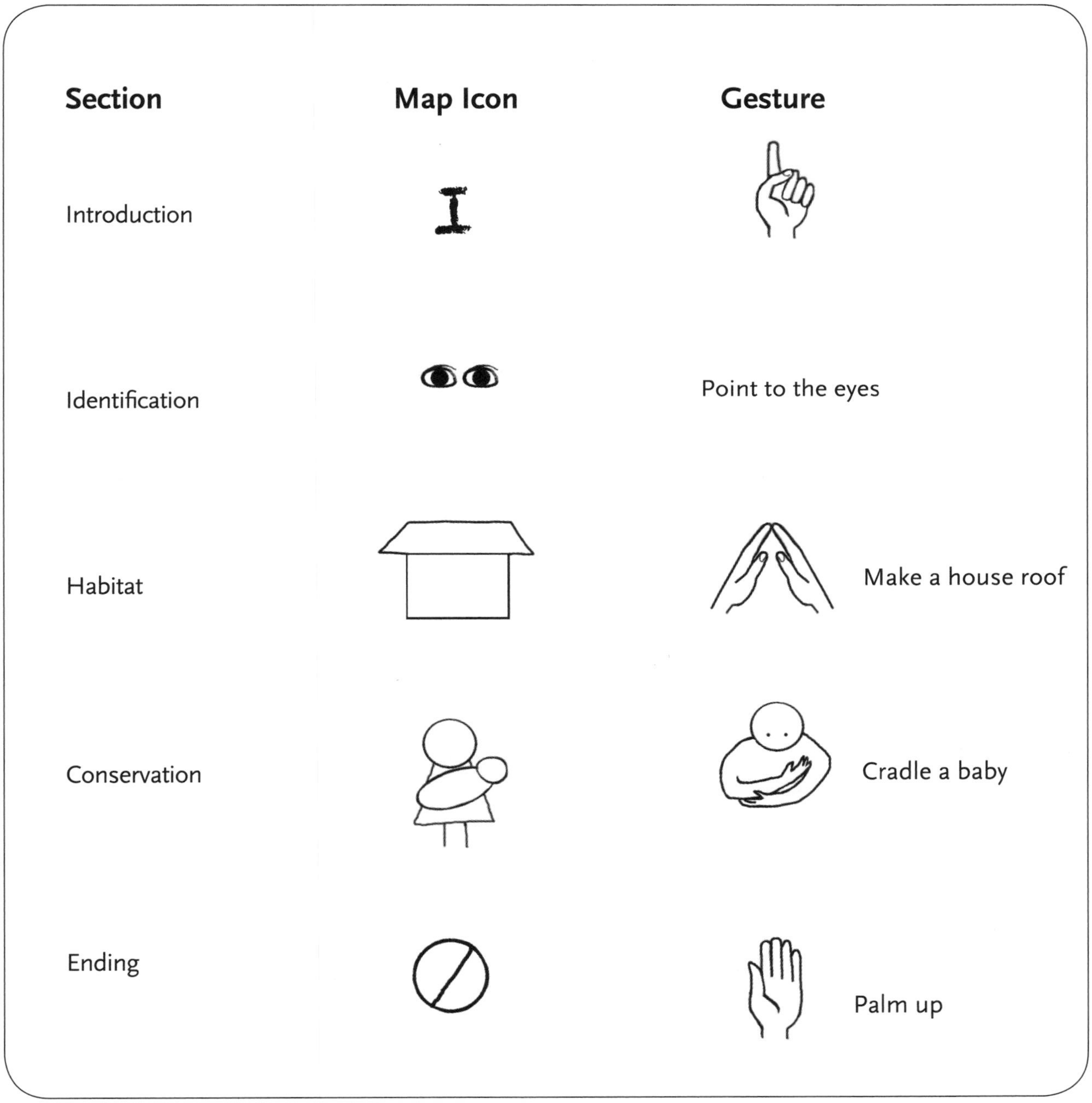

Section	Map Icon	Gesture
Introduction	I	
Identification	👀	Point to the eyes
Habitat		Make a house roof
Conservation		Cradle a baby
Ending	⊘	Palm up

Then you could create a map with some of the detail listed in sequence. It might look like this:

Notice with this map there is more detail than with a typical story map, though less than with the 'word map'. It's fine if they change the wording a bit so long as they keep the main points and any key language features you want them to use. They can step first from the map, then without the map, before practising telling in the same way. Try and get a gesture for each step where possible.

1.2 Deepening

Once the piece can be told from memory you can use many of the exercises in the deepening chapter to use and develop the language. For example you might:

➤ Role-play a Jub-Jub bird presentation to a conference by an expert

➤ Role-play a conversation about the bird between a friend who saw it and one who didn't

➤ Draw a picture of the Jub-Jub bird labelling its main features and present/explain to partner and class

➤ Role-play a TV debate about ways to preserve Jub-Jub birds

➤ Role-play/enact claw seller trying to sell claws to undercover reporter

➤ Write a song about the Jub-Jub bird

➤ Create a play about the conservation of the bird

➤ Create and perform Jub-Jub bird poems

You could also show the class other examples of similar types of texts at this time, as suggested in the warm-ups section – model texts and clips about birds, 'magpie' ideas and structures you might use later.

The main point is to make it fun, satisfying and motivating: make it memorable!

Any of these exercises can be linked to a short piece of writing if you wish.

1.3 Talk about the structure and language

After this it might be a good time to go back to the imitated piece, maybe read it and talk about it with the class, looking at the purpose, structure and language features that they might consider using in their own versions.

If you haven't already, now you might box up the text or map into sections, just like you can do with stories. It might look something like this:

Section
Introduction
Identification
Habitat
Conservation
Ending

Explain the purpose of each section, list together the useful phrases and words used and put them on your working wall or washing line. Pie Corbett and Julia Strong's book *Talk for Writing Across the Curriculum* is great for this, setting out common words and phrases that can be used for the different kinds of text. They suggest creating a 'toolkit' for each particular text type of key language and structural features, which can then be used to guide innovation, invention and shared writing. This could be developed and explained to the class at this stage.

Innovation

At the oral innovation stage we re-use the imitated idea, changing elements of content while keeping the same basic structure. Just as with fiction, we can substitute, add and delete elements of the piece or recycle the whole structure.

You have lots of choices about different ways to innovate orally. For example:

➤ You could stick with the theme of the Jub-Jub bird and add, delete and substitute elements of the piece to make it even better

➤ You could recycle the structure of the piece and apply it to a new fantasy, fictional or real-life bird.

It's the same basic process as spelt out in Chapter 6. First demonstrate with the class using *shared innovation,* then have the students work independently or in groups to create their own innovations.

Shared innovation

Working with a boxed up structure you can get the class to create ideas for changing each section, collecting ideas and then choosing the ones to include. It might look like this:

Section	Ideas
Introduction	Interesting fact – smallest
Identification	Tiny silver wings, two heads, curved beaks, funny smell
Habitat	Under the roots of the Tum-Tum tree in burrows of the Fu-Fu bunny
Conservation	Needed to pollinate flowers of Tum-Tum tree. Now Fu-Fu bunnies are rare as they are being hunted by the field mice militia
Ending	Interdependence. Should bunny hunting be allowed?

Then you might demonstrate how to create a word map, step it through and retell the piece using their new ideas. In this way you model re-using the phrases, patterns and structures in a new version of the piece and show them how to retell it.

You might get a piece like this:

The Fu-Fu bird

Did you know that the Fu-Fu bird is the smallest bird in the world?

It can easily be distinguished by its tiny size and distinctive shape. Mature birds are about the size of a fly with four pairs of silver wings and two sharp pointed heads. Their two tiny beaks are curved like little bananas, while their claws are like little thorns. Female Fu-Fu birds smell like marzipan, while males smell like hot fudge.

And so on ...

Independent innovation

Now you can let individuals or small groups go through the same process using their ideas to create a new piece, mapping stepping and retelling in various ways until you feel the ideas are ready. If you wish, you can move into writing using these ideas.

Invention

Here, invention means applying the pattern and language of the non-fiction piece to a new subject, requiring adaptation and modification.

For example, you might look at creating an information piece about the Freedom Bird using the information in the story, or a piece about real-life birds, or maybe pieces about other animals. In this way the students get used to creating suitable information pieces about animals in different ways.

Usually you will need to demonstrate invention with the class before asking them to have a go by themselves. Here's an example of teaching sequence for creating an information piece about birds. Let's say you will demonstrate making up a piece about eagles, and then have them apply the same approach independently to other kinds of birds.

Shared invention

You might start by presenting some ideas and facts about eagles for the class to work from. Next you can brainstorm a suitable structure (boxed up grid) for your piece with the class. You might come up with:

> Introduction

> Appearance

> Habitat

> Feeding

> Life cycle

> Conservation

> Ending

Then you can decide together about the content of each section before showing them mapping, stepping and speaking based on that content.

Independent invention

Now you can ask individuals or small groups to go through the same process for different birds. You might give them a fact sheet or have them conduct their own research for the piece. Just as with the previous example, once they have mapped and stepped, give plenty of time for telling and improving before you move on to writing if you wish.

Shared and independent writing

Once you have completed the oral telling stage for imitation, innovation or invention, you may then want to link this to a piece of writing, so the class practises translating all their words and ideas into writing. All the previous exercises can be seen as a rehearsal, so when the students get around to writing their ideas and plans are really clear, and they can concentrate on getting them down on paper rather than wondering what to write.

So you may choose to:

➤ Write from an imitated piece

➤ Write from an innovated piece

➤ Write from an invented piece

Either way the suggested process is much the same as set out in Chapter 8: first demonstrate creating a new text by boxing up the structure and taking suggestions for words and sentences for each section, then edit and improve the text together.

They can then have a go at independent writing using your demonstration as a guide.

Here's an example of shared writing to create an innovated text from the original Jub-Jub bird piece.

Example of shared writing for innovated text

Let's say you have worked on innovations to the Jub-Jub bird story by creating oral versions for various other mythic birds. Now you can move to writing. Just as with shared writing for fiction you are demonstrating the process of generate-reflect-select. Just as with shared writing for fiction you can decide how closely to stick to the language features of the original text and how far to invent new ones with the class.

So box up the structure of the text like this:

If you have a teaching assistant you may ask him/her to scribe all the ideas up on a working wall. You can also ask students to make notes of their favourite ideas for future use in their notebooks. This is all intended to give them lots of ideas when they get to writing.

And then you might say:

Do you remember how we created a piece called the Fu-Fu bird last week? Well now we are going to write a text about the Fu-Fu bird as an entry in the handbook of mythic birds.

Next decide whether to keep the main wording of the original text and change the content (single word or phrase suggestions) or whether to get the class to draft whole sentences in any way they want.

For single words you might say:

OK in the Jub-Jub bird text the first sentence says: Did you know that the Jub-Jub bird is the heaviest flying creature in the world? Now we are writing about the Fu-Fu bird.

Let's start our sentence in the same way with:

Did you know that the Fu-Fu bird is the .....

Section/Paragraph Heading	Text
Introduction	
Identification	
Habitat	
Conservation	
Ending	

What idea could we use to catch the reader's attention?

Or if we want to give more options to our class we could say:

In the Jub-Jub text we start with a question and interesting fact to grab the reader's attention. What question might you start with for the Fu-Fu bird?

Or to pitch it even wider you might just ask them to think of a good opening hook sentence.

Either way, take suggestions, chart them all up on the working wall so others can use them, then choose which to use for the class text and write it up (or have the class choose in some way).

In this way you can create the first draft of the innovated text together. You might then edit it with the class for content and then for grammar, spelling and punctuation. In all cases take the class's suggestions and choose which ones to adopt.

You might end up with something like this, if the text is followed closely:

The Fu-Fu bird

Did you know that the Fu-Fu bird is the tiniest bird in the world?

It's really easy to identify as it is very small and a very unusual shape. Mature birds are about 1 cm long with eight silver wings and two sharp conical heads with three eyes on each. Their two tiny beaks are curved like little bananas, while their claws are small and sharp. Female Fu-Fu birds give off the smell of marzipan when trying to attract a mate. The males always smell like hot fudge.

And so on ...

Independent innovation

Once you have created and edited your text you can ask the class to write their own versions, using the same task sequence that you demonstrated in shared writing: i.e. box it up, draft ideas for each box, draft a paragraph for each box and edit. You can pause this process for oral rehearsals and pairs sharing every now and then to keep the process fluid and engaging. Once their first text has been generated have the class review and improve their work in pairs, small groups and whole class sessions.

Example: shared writing for invented text

Let's say you have worked with the class to create oral versions of information pieces on various birds. In just the same way as for invention we can now translate all those ideas into text, first by modelling and then with independent work.

You might create a text about eagles with your class, drawing on the work you did together in the oral stage.

Let's say you have developed this format at the oral stage:

➤ Introduction

➤ Appearance

➤ Habitat

➤ Feeding

➤ Life cycle

➤ Conservation

➤ Ending

Now you can work through the sections together, sentence-by-sentence, creating a draft text, followed by a shared edit. Remember to read the piece out loud frequently to help the class focus on what is working and what needs improvement in the whole text.

You might end up with something like this:

Example of information text about eagles	
Introduction	Have you ever seen an eagle hovering in the sky, searching for prey, then dive to the ground like a rocket, catching its prey in its claws and flying off again in the blink of an eye? If you have you may understand why many consider them to be the most magnificent birds in the world.
Appearance	Eagles are large, powerfully built birds of prey, with a heavy head and beak. Like all birds of prey, eagles have very large hooked beaks for tearing flesh from their prey, strong muscular legs, and powerful claws. The largest eagle in the world has a wingspan of more than 2 metres. The heaviest weighs more than six kilograms. Eagles' eyes are extremely powerful, which enables them to spot potential prey from a very long distance. This keen eyesight is primarily because of their large pupils.
Habitat	Eagles normally build their nests in tall trees or on high cliffs. They usually live far away from human habitation in isolated places. Some live in forests, some live in mountains and others by the sea. It depends on their diet and where they can find food and be safe. The majority of eagles live in Asia and Africa. Only one species, the golden eagle, can be found in the UK.
Feeding	Due to the size and power of many eagle species, they are ranked at the top of the food chain in the bird world. The type of prey varies from eagle to eagle. The majority eat mammals; however some eat fish, some eat snakes and others feed on smaller birds. Most eagles grab prey without landing and take flight with it so the prey can be carried to a perch and torn apart.
Life cycle	Many species lay two eggs, but the older, larger chick frequently kills its younger sibling once it has hatched. The dominant chick tends to be the female, as they are bigger than the male. The parents take no action to stop the killing.
Conservation	Every year there are fewer and fewer eagles in the world. There are many reasons for this. In the past eagles have been killed by farmers who feel they are a danger to their animals. Also people sometimes steal and sell their eggs to collectors for high prices. Finally the use of pesticides in farming has led to the death of many eagles. In the UK there are only a few golden eagles left.
Ending	The eagle is top of the food chain, which means that no other creature will hunt the eagle for food. Scientists have noticed that most other birds of prey look around over their shoulder just before a kill to check if there are enemies about. However, apparently the eagle never looks around in this way. Maybe that's why the eagle is known as the king of the birds.

After that let them follow the same process alone or in pairs on their own chosen birds. You might include various deepening exercises and role-play games before creating a draft plan and then independently creating text. You can use HMSS to remember the overall structure and main points in each section, or text mapping if you want to learn it word-for-word.

Sometimes, to keep engagement, the teaching needs to be broken down into small chunks of independent writing linked to demonstrations and feedback. Sometimes the class may learn more by extended periods of uninterrupted writing. As a teacher you can adapt the sequencing of modelling and independent writing depending on the needs of your class as they develop.

Independent innovation requires students to develop their own planning skills. You might try using a planning form like the one below for them to get used to that process.

Planning form for non-fiction invention

Purpose:

Audience:

Author/Speaker:

Title:

Section/Paragraph	Purpose	Ideas

Questions needing more research:

Cross-curricular application

Now whenever information reports or presentations about animals come up in other areas of the curriculum students may remember and re-use the report patterns they have learned. For information texts about other topics they will apply the same principles but may have to develop or be given a different structure to work from.

Mix and match these techniques

Within the overall scheme of warm-up, imitate, innovate and invent there are lots of different ways to teach. Some teachers stay longer with warm-ups and oral development. Others go more quickly to writing and focus less on the oral stages. That's up to you, depending on what you want to teach and the attitudes and preferences of your class. The main thing is to make it fun and affirming so you can help the students build confidence in their own capacity to generate new ideas and then turn them into presentations, performances and pieces of writing.

Teaching tips summary

> Use oral warm-ups and exercises, not just to help with writing but because these skills really matter

> Use texts and topics that you like and that your students will find exciting

> Use fantasy to teach structure before working with factual content: it's much easier

> Don't forget the main point is to produce an effective presentation or a great piece of writing. Keep that focus and use language features to achieve this, not the other way round

> Weave in ways to read and discuss model texts and put the good bits up on your working wall for all to use

> Just as with fiction, list the purpose of each section before drafting and then check back against the purpose

> Check also that the whole links together in a coherent way

> Make sure you find ways to celebrate suggestions and completed pieces for writing in various ways so achievement can be witnessed and affirmed.

Chapter 9   Non-fiction: Six types of communication

Chapter 10

Curriculum integration

Introduction

In order to become a Storytelling School you will have to decide how stories will be linked into the curriculum across the whole school. Different schools plan in different ways. There is no single model or scheme. The main thing is that the approach is thought through, communicated clearly to all teaching staff, who need to be provided with suitable resources to get the job done.

Often the school will develop its approach step by step, starting with a set of stories for teaching narrative, and then adding in non-fiction teaching before expanding the storytelling to include a range of other subjects. This approach has the advantage of getting teachers used to the approach in one area first. It is usually best to start with traditional fiction stories as they are easiest and most fun. Once staff have tried it out and gained confidence, the rest is much easier. One teacher put it like this: 'Once you've got the hang of storytelling it makes teaching anything so much easier. Just start with a story and work from there.'

In this chapter we present a few popular ways of integrating storytelling into the curriculum in Storytelling Schools. Feel free to imitate, innovate and invent as you see fit.

First we will look at literacy planning across the school, and then discuss examples from history, personal and social education, religion, science and music.

The main point is: plan and support across the whole school so students experience a consistent and systematic approach to learning. Find great stories and your staff and students will be happier, more engaged and will learn efficiently and effectively.

When asked what he thought about the storytelling method in a school where it was newly adopted, an enthusiastic child said:

'I like it 'cos it's better than work.'

His results improved dramatically.

In this chapter we will look at curriculum integration for:

➤ Literacy

➤ History

➤ Personal and Social Education

➤ Religion

➤ Science

➤ Music

Literacy

Whole school story curriculum

To become a Storytelling School you need to have a storytelling curriculum. This means a list of stories, which the children will learn every year. This is to avoid duplication between years and achieve a progression in story level as the student moves through the school.

Most Storytelling Schools teach at least six stories a year: one every half term. This story is then learned at the beginning of term and used as a basis for teaching literacy during that term. This means that during a six-year stay at the school the student will learn at least 36 stories. That's a respectable repertoire to carry through into later life.

Many primary schools work around what they call a creative curriculum, meaning a lead topic or theme every half term. Most teaching in that half term is then linked one way or another to that topic. Storytelling Schools with a creative curriculum often find stories linked to these topics so that the topic itself can be retained.

The table opposite shows an early example of this approach from SS Mary and John's Primary in Oxford, the first school we know of which adopted this approach. The idea proved popular and spread fast.

In this section we will cover:

➤ Story curriculum

➤ Linking with creative curriculum

➤ Linking with literary curriculum

➤ Linking to the basic plots

➤ Whole school stories

➤ Non-fiction links

➤ Language and narrative progressions

➤ Sample teaching plans

➤ Reading

➤ Poetry

Key to books:

100WM: *100 World Myths and Legends* by Geraldine McCaughrean (Orion)

ST: *The Story Tree* by Hugh Lupton (Barefoot)

TWW: *Tales of Wisdom and Wonder* by Hugh Lupton (Barefoot)

AT: *Animal Tales from Around the World* by Naomi Adler (Barefoot)

RTT: *Ready-to-Tell Tales* by David Holt and Bill Mooney (August House)

MRTT: *More Ready-to-Tell Tales* by David Holt and Bill Mooney (August House)

WIF: *West Indian Folk Tales* retold by Philip Sherlock (OUP)

100GS: *Britannia 100 Great Stories* by Geraldine McCaughrean (Dolphin)

OIS: *Our Island Story* by H. Marshall (Phoenix)

IY: *The Islamic Year* by Chris Smith (Hawthorn Press)

EM: *Egyptian Myths* by Jacqueline Morley (Hodder Wayland)

	Autumn 1	Autumn 2	Spring 1	Spring 2	Summer 1	Summer 2
Year 1	Humans and animals	Houses and homes	Toys	Pushes and pulls – forces	The world around us – sounds	Eating and growing
	Monkey and Papa God (Haiti) TWW	*The Sweetest Song (African-American) TWW*	*The Wooden Baby*	*B'Whale and B'Elephant (Bahamas) MRTT*	*The Noisy House (World) 100WM*	*Little Red Hen (English) ST*
Year 2	History detectives	An island setting	Pakistan	People who help us	Seaside holidays	Minibeasts
	Charles II – how London burned (English History) OIS	*Call of the Sea (Channel Islands) 100WM*	*The Birth of the Prophet (Trad Islamic) IY*	*Sweet and Sour Berries (China) MRTT*	*Sedna and King Gull (Canada) AT*	*Grandmother Spider (Native American) AT/MRTT*
Year 3	Sounds	Materials – evaporating and dissolving	Mythical monsters	Plants	Egypt – past and present	Humans and animals
	How music was fetched out of heaven (Aztec) 100WM	*First Snow (Native American) 100WM*	*George and the Dragon (Iran) 100WM*	*John Barleycorn (Traditional American) 100WM*	*RA the Shining One (ancient Egypt) EM*	*The Curing Fox (Native American) TWW*
Year 4	Romans	Hinduism	Winter	Other cultures – India	Habitats	Oxford castle
	Cupid and Psyche (ancient Roman) 100WM	*Monkey Do Hanuman (India) 100WM*	*The Piper's Revenge (Scotland) MRTT*	*The Armchair Traveller (India) 100WM*	*Magic in the Rainforest (Brazil) AT*	*Matilda (trad Oxford)*
Year 5	Tudors	People	Carnival	Plants	Rivers	Coasts
	Henry VIII and 6 Wives (UK History) OIS	*The Blue Coat (Jewish) ST*	*Anansi and the Bag of Stories (Caribbean) WIF*	*Proud Man (Native American) 100WM*	*Singer above the River (Germany) 100WM*	*Mary and the Seal (Scotland) MRTT*
Year 6	WWII	Islam	Challenging stereotypes	Africa	Japanese culture	Mountain environment
	The Brave Little Boats of Dunkirk 100GS	*Nest and Web (Islam) 100WM*	*Blind Man and the Hunter (Africa) TWW*	*The Black Prince (Egypt) RTT*	*Biggest (Japan) 100WM*	*The Unlucky Mountain (British) MRTT*

To develop your own story curriculum, selecting the right stories is important. If you are matching the stories up to topics, you need to find suitable stories for that theme. Different schools do this in different ways:

> *147 Traditional Stories for Primary School Children to Retell* (Hawthorn Press) has proved popular as it has an index of topics and stories matched up for easy reference

> The Story Museum website has a useful database of stories also classified by topics, and you can hear the stories online, which speeds up learning them

> Search the internet using 'traditional story' and the theme can create great and unexpected options

> Some schools ask a storyteller to help out by suggesting suitable stories

> Some schools get the teachers themselves to find suitable stories

> Swapping story ideas in staff meetings is a good way to pool knowledge of tried and tested stories

> Adapt known picture books/short stories which link to a theme for oral storytelling

Once a draft curriculum has been created it is usually important to run the stories past the teachers to check if they like them or if they have alternative suggestions. It's best if your teachers love the stories they tell, so that they can pass on their inspiration to their class. Also, when the teachers are getting started it's good to coach or peer practise their storytelling both to build confidence and reduce the risk of the teacher just reading the story or showing a clip of it.

Some schools have a literature-based curriculum with a lead book to read and study each term linked in to literacy and cross-curricular teaching. When these schools become Storytelling Schools they need to find a way to integrate the storytelling elements too. Some keep the focus on a half-termly book and ensure

that there is also at least one story per half term that is learned orally and worked with in the way described in this book. Some of the books, especially in KS1, will be good for storytelling too and so can be used both for reading and storytelling. Others are unsuitable for telling and there the school has to find a traditional story that has a theme connected to the book.

Some novellas and novels can be told orally, requiring the breakdown of the overall story into a simpler core narrative of a single main plot line. Storytellers can help draft a summary suitable for oral retelling if needed.

Another option is to start the school year with a 'whole school story', which is worked with across the whole school for the first few weeks of term. This can generate a lot of excitement about the story with lots of possibilities for work between year groups and whole school events. It also serves to illustrate for all staff how easily any story can be adapted to suit a particular age, and is also a good way to introduce new staff to the system.

One innovative school has extended this approach to the whole year. They have six stories a year for the whole school and everyone works with each story for one term, then a new set of six for the next year, and so on for a six-year cycle. They say it works really well.

If you want to be a Storytelling School then you need a storytelling curriculum to ensure that storytelling is used systematically to teach literacy. Our experience is that otherwise it is really hard to adopt a consistent whole-school approach.

Integrating non-fiction

Another popular way of planning literacy is to decide on a non-fiction focus and text for each half term and work with this using the storytelling methods. As there are six types of non-fiction communication (see previous chapter) this is quite handy because it means that the classes can cover one type per half term and all six every year, so that by year six they will have focused on each type of non-fiction six times and hopefully got the hang of it.

The theme and text may be linked to the story explicitly (say a discussion text, should the wolf be punished?) or linked to its theme (for example, the bird theme linked to *The Freedom Song*). Sometimes a new non-linked text is used where that seems better. You can mix and match in various ways.

Often the first half of a typical six-week half term is allocated to teaching the fiction story and the second half to the non-fiction focus. This can allow all the imagination, enthusiasm and rich vocabulary from the storytelling to be channelled into the non-fiction unit.

On the following two pages is an example of such a curriculum plan from Temple Cowley Primary School in Oxford. It also features a whole school story in term 1 and classifies the stories used by plot type (see below) and the non-fiction topics by non-fiction type. They have also squeezed in a few weeks for their poetry teaching.

Yr 1 and 2 a

	Term 1 (8 weeks)			Term 2 (7 weeks)			Term 3 (6 weeks)		Term 4 (6 weeks)		Term 5 (5 weeks)		Term 6 (7 weeks)		
	2 wks N	3 wks N	3 wks NF	3 wks N	3 wks NF	1 wk P	3 wks N	3 wks NF	3 wks N	3 wks NF	2.5 wks N	2.5 wks NF	2 wks P	2.5 wks N	2.5 wks NF
Whole school story	Samuel Pepys			Castles			Ocean world		Take one book		Light and dark		Joseph		
		The great fire of London / *Historical/Overcoming the monster*	Jack's diary / *Recount*	William and Harold / *Historical Tragedy*	How to make/defend a castle / *Instructions*	Unit 1	Smiley Shark / *Voyage and return*	Under the sea/Sharks / *Non-chron report*	Take one book: Three Little Pigs / *Tragedy*	Adverts / *Persuasive*	Peace at Last / *Comedy*	How day and night occur? How a bulb lights up? / *Explanation*	Unit 2	Joseph / *Rebirth*	Should Joseph help his brothers? / *Discussion*

Yr 1 and 2 b

	2 wks N	3 wks N	3 wks NF	3 wks N	3 wks NF	1 wk P	3 wks N	3 wks NF	3 wks N	3 wks NF	2.5 wks N	2.5 wks NF	2 wks P	2.5 wks N	2.5 wks NF
Whole school story	Edmund Hillary			Victorians			Rainforests		Space		Bees		Hinduism / SATs		
		The story of Edmund Hillary / *Voyage and return*	How to drive a dog sledge / *Instructions*	The Ugly Duckling / *Rebirth*	My trip to the Victorian Museum / *Recount*	Unit 1	Poetry Unit 2 / The Jungle Book	All about Jaguars / *Non-chron report*	Whatever Next / *Voyage and return*	Adverts for space equipment / *Voyage and return*	Winnie the Pooh / The Hungry Caterpillar / *Voyage and return*	How bees make honey / *Explanation*	Narrative: Take one picture	Narrative: Ganesh and Kartikiya / *Voyage and return*	Did Ganesh Cheat? / *Discussion*

Yr 3

	Term 1 (8 weeks)			Term 2 (7 weeks)			Term 3 (6 weeks)		Term 4 (6 weeks)		Term 5 (5 weeks)		Term 6 (7 weeks)		
	2 wks N	3 wks N	3 wks NF	3 wks N	3 wks NF	1 wk P	3 wks N	3 wks NF	3 wks N	3 wks NF	2.5 wks N	2.5 wks NF	2 wks P	2.5 wks N	2.5 wks NF
Whole school story	Henry VIII			Light and lighthouses			Ancient Egypt		Parlez-vous français?		Take one book		Weddings		
		The story of Anne Boleyn / *Tragedy/Historical*	Henry's diary / *Recount*	The lighthouse keeper's lunch / *Overcoming the monster*	How a lighthouse works / *Explanation*	Unit 1	Egyptian Cinderella / *Rags to riches*	Mummification / *Non-chron report*	Beauty and the beast / *Rebirth*	How to make French food / *Instructions*	The Minpins / *Overcoming the monster*	Suction boots/house / *Persuasive adverts*	Unit 2	When Willy went to the wedding / *Comedy*	Do you agree with marriage? / *Discussion*

Yr 4

	2 wks N	3 wks N	3 wks NF	3 wks N	3 wks NF	1 wk P	3 wks N	3 wks NF	3 wks N	3 wks NF	2.5 wks N	2.5 wks NF	2 wks P	2.5 wks N	2.5 wks NF
Whole school story	Roger Bannister			Space and beyond			Aztecs		Volcanoes		Habitats: Take one book		Guru Nanak		
		Roger Bannister's story / *Overcoming the monster*	How to run a mile in under 4 minutes / *Instructions*	Space adventure story/ Dinosaurs and all that rubbish / *Rebirth*	Aliens / *Non-chron report*	Unit 1	The Ragpicker and the Priest / *Rags to riches*	Adverts / *Persuasive*	Escape from Pompeii / *Tragedy/Historical*	Newspaper reports / *Recount*	Tuesday and The Hodgeheg / *Quest*	How a tadpole turns into a frog / *Explanation*	Unit 2	The Crocodile and the Priest / *Rebirth*	Should we have school rules? / *Discussion*

		Term 1 (8 weeks)			Term 2 (7 weeks)			Term 3 (6 weeks)		Term 4 (6 weeks)		Term 5 (5 weeks)		Term 6 (7 weeks)		
		2 wks N	3 wks N	3 wks NF	3 wks N	3 wks NF	1 wk P	3 wks N	3 wks NF	3 wks N	3 wks NF	2.5 wks N	2.5 wks NF	2 wks P	2.5 wks N	2.5 wks NF
Yr 5	Whole school story	Martin Luther King			Australia			Anglo-Saxons/Vikings		In the garden		Rivers		Mountains/Buddhism		
			Journey to Jo'berg (Book) *Voyage and return*	'I have a dream' speech *Persuasive (speech)*	Take one book There's a boy in the girl's bathroom (book) *Rebirth*	All about Kangaroos (any Australian animal) *Non-chron report*	Unit 1 Christmas Russian poetry / songs	Beowulf *Overcoming the monster*	Letters to other characters in the story *Recount*	Bad Tempered Ladybird *Voyage and return*	How to care for plants *Instructions*	The Selkie Story *Tragedy*	How rivers are formed *Explanation*	Unit 2 Sensational	Touching the Void *Voyage and return*	Was he right to cut the rope? *Discussion*
Yr 6	Whole school story	John Lennon			May the force be with you			WW2 Take one book		Oxford		Short film		The Odyssey Ancient Greece		
			John Lennon *Recount: biography/autobiography*	School council *Persuasive*	Sci fi/hover bike *Narrative*	Space *Non-chron reports Instructions Explanation: through science*	Christmas	Goodnight Mr Tom *Rebirth*	The Blitz *Newspaper reports: recount*	Alice in Wonderland/ The Jabberwocky *Voyage and return*	Temple Cowley Pool *Discussion*	The Piano/dangle	SATS *(exam prep)*	The Highwayman	Odysseus and Cyclops *Overcoming the monster*	

Key: **N** = Narrative
NF = Non-fiction
P = Poetry

Plot types

A third popular way to set out a story curriculum is to include a spread of plot types in every year so that the students can get to know all the plots by covering a variety every year (see the seven basic plots in Chapter 7). One way to look for suitable stories is by using the second volume in this series: *147 Traditional Stories for Primary School Children to Retell* (Hawthorn Press) where stories are classified by plot type.

Using narrative and language progressions

Many schools systematically link their storytelling and story writing to a whole school language learning strategy so that a progression of language features are learned through storytelling from Foundation through to Year 6.

Below is an example of a progression from Pie Corbett. The basic idea is that each year in the school the teacher should consolidate all the previous language features and introduce a few new ones. The language modelled in the storytelling and story writing can then incorporate these features.

Foundation	Year 1	Year 2
Once upon a time	After/after that	After a while
Early one morning	One day	A moment later
And	At the moment	The next day
Then	Soon/as soon as	However
Next	Because	After
Until/till	Suddenly	Meanwhile
But	By the next morning	When it was all over
So	To his amazement	... to ...
Finally	In the end	More adjectives
... happily ever after	First	Adverbs: eventually, unluckily
... who ...	... that ...	Simile using 'like'
'Run' (he walked and he walked...)	... or ...	Sentence with three descriptors
Description: a lean cat, a mean cat ...	... so that ...	
Alliteration	... when ...	
Adverbs: luckily/unfortunately	... where ...	
Prepositions: down, into, over, out, onto	Repetition for effect	
	Adjectives to describe	
	Simile using 'as'	
	Adverbs: suddenly, immediately	
	Prepositions: inside, towards	

In addition, as well as language features, some schools spell out the kind of imitation, innovation and invention that students are expected to master every year, together with the narrative elements from the curriculum that the students are expected to learn. This helps the teachers to clarify in more detail what they are expected to teach every year, how it all links up with previous and future years, and how it links to the overall curriculum goals for narrative. This can also help teachers explain the purpose and context of the storytelling approach during inspections. This is important because many teachers can feel anxious that they will be judged poorly during these inspections if they try new ideas. The framework helps build confidence and consistency.

Some schools work from a useful framework developed by Carol Satterthwaite with a group of schools in Bradford, editing and revising it to suit their own needs. You can find the scheme on the Story Museum website to download free.

Year 3 & 4	Year 5 & 6
Later	Elaborate starter like 'Early one first morning …'
Whenever	Although
Without warning	If
Eventually	-ed clause starter
-ing clause starter: 'Running alone, Tim ...	-ed drop in clause
Drop in -ing clause: 'Tim, running along, tripped over'	Sentence with three actions: 'Tim ran home, sat down and drank his tea.'
Short sentences, questions, exclamations	Speech plus stage directions: 'Stop,' he whispered, picking up his tea.
Speech	

Term plans

Teachers have to work out how to organise their literacy teaching week by week, adjusting to the aptitudes and learning needs of their class. There is no single format for this: it depends how much time your class needs to master each step, and which particular narrative and non-fiction elements you will be focusing on. The following gives an example of a possible way of sequencing teaching during a term, for both the fiction and non-fiction elements, for a 15-hour teaching plan.

This does not include short warm-ups, story games, language games and cross-curricular links that can be used liberally through that period as well. Please do not copy these: they are only for illustration. Make up your own depending on what you have to teach.

The basic pattern will probably begin as:

➤ **Week 1** learn and deepen the story including poetry (5 hours)

➤ **Week 2** shared writing of various sections into complete text (5 hours)

➤ **Week 3** innovate, retell and rewrite; or invent, tell, and write (5 hours)

You can then innovate from this.

1. Storytelling and narrative with innovation writing	
Time in hours	Activity
1	Tell , map and step (communal)
1	Map, step and tellings (independent)
1	Refine and develop independent tellings in groups and to class
1	Shared innovation – model specific innovation and map and step
1	Independent innovation (I) children map and step their own innovations
1	Independent innovation (2) refine and develop story ideas
1	Deepening of innovated stories – drama or writing activity
1	Shared writing of section of innovated text
1	Shared and independent writing of sections followed by independent writing of same section for child's story
2	Editing and revisions in small peer groups
1	Completion, celebration, re-enactment of texts
1	Invention: shared invention of story
1	Create own oral version of own story from stimulus including mapping and stepping
1	Write up invented story

Total: 15 hours

2. Storytelling and narrative with short writing assignments and big write of imitated story

Time in hours	Activity
1	(Tell) Hear , map, step and tell (independent)
1	Refine telling (pairs, groups, to class)
2	Deepening: role-play phone home then write diary entry
2	Deepening: narrative poem then write up
2	Deepening: role-play press conference then newspaper article
2	Deepening: enact sections in groups, then write quick drama script
3	Shared and independent writing of imitated story, section by section
2	Invention using same basic plot and quick write-up

Total: 15 hours

3. Non-fiction unit

Time in hours	Activity
1	Warm up the communication focus with role-play and texts
1	Shared mapping and stepping: learn the sample text communally
1	Independent mapping and stepping: learn to tell in pairs
2	Deepening
3	Shared and independent innovation
4	Shared and independent writing
3	Independent applications

Total: 15 hours

Integrating reading

There are various ways that reading can be linked to the storytelling scheme:

First, once students have mastered HMSS they can try Read Map Step Speak (RMSS): After reading the story they then map, step and tell it. Where there is enthusiasm for telling this gives reading purpose.

Second, there are various ways to include reading in the deepening stage of the storytelling:

➤ Students can read one or more written versions of the story and include some of the language in their oral telling. You may also discuss the texts with them, exploring the techniques which the author uses, to help them 'read like a writer'.

➤ Students can read texts relevant to the story to develop their understanding of elements of the story.

➤ Students can do web research looking at particular elements of the story.

Third, at the innovation stage students may read various versions and retellings of the story and incorporate elements into their own innovations.

Fourth, students can be asked to find their own stories linked to topics through web and library research.

Critique and comprehension

Pupils within a Storytelling School where basic plots have been taught alongside an understanding of how the story matrix works in the creation of new stories, have a much deeper insight into the structure of narratives within books. Their knowledge of these plots and structures inform their critique of books, enabling them to identify familiar patterns and give them the vocabulary they need to express their observations. Pupils can talk about books using technical terms: 'This book is essentially a tragedy,' or 'The story is driven by the hero's "quest" or "calling"'. They will also be able to identify the functions key characters play in the books they read and offer suggestions as to the purpose and role that they play. The process of shared writing and 'thinking like writers' draws pupils' attention to the key questions that writers ask themselves to create characters and the fact that they might be striving to 'show' and not 'tell them' things. In this way, the whole storymaking process is so integrated with the writer and the reader, that the interplay between them can always be connected, enriching critique and comprehension. To put it simply, as storytellers we think of our audience, as writers we think of our reader and as readers we empathise with the hypothetic desires of the writer whose words we perceive in our own unique and personal way. All the disciplines feed into and enrich each other. It's a perfect marriage!

Poetry

Many Storytelling Schools link their poetry teaching to their storytelling, often at the deepening stage where the story is explored and developed in a variety of ways. Poetry is a great way to do this, creating new ways of expressing parts of the story and its whole. Some of these poetic ideas can be recycled back into the retelling and writing of the story.

Poetry-making can be thought of in exactly the same way as storymaking:

➤ Poems may be learned by heart (imitate)

➤ The form and language of the poem can then be adapted and applied to a new context (innovation)

➤ Poems may be freely invented based on known patterns and rules or none

➤ The enthusiasm that telling a story creates can be channelled into poetry-making too

Here are some examples of ways to integrate poetry into the storytelling curriculum:

➤ Poems can be learned using hear, map, step, speak and/or text mapping

➤ Narrative poems can be retold as stories before being learned as poems

➤ At the deepening stage of any story poems in any format can be created from the material in the story

➤ Poems can be created to retell a whole story

➤ Poems can be used as a stimulus for story invention

➤ Stories (scenes/settings/characters) can be used as a stimulus for writing poems

➤ Poems/songs can be invented to add to a story

➤ Poems linked to the theme of the story may be read during deepening and the ideas used in the retellings

Poetry is a great way to explore the use of language in stories, enabling a 'raising the level' of the language used in the story. Traditionally many stories were recited through poetry. It's a time-honoured tradition and works really well. All types of poems to be covered in the curriculum can be integrated in this way.

History

History is all about retelling, explaining and discussing what has happened in the past. This makes history topics great for storytelling because history is all about time lines, characters and events and how they all fit together, just like stories. This means there are loads of ways to weave the storytelling toolkit into history teaching.

Some schools with a topic-led curriculum do this by choosing a historical topic for that term and then choosing a relevant story to work on both in literacy and as a starting point for looking at the history element. Other schools will have discrete history topics and find time to tell and learn a relevant story as an introduction to the particular history topic.

Whatever the system, stories in history provide a great opportunity for enquiry-based learning, where students explore and investigate the questions of interest to them in the story.

Students may then use the six types of non-fiction to present their findings orally and/or in writing, including recount, discussion and explanation.

Here are a few common examples of stories that are used to introduce a theme:

➤ Boudicca and the Romans

➤ William, Harold and 1066

➤ Canute and Alfred

➤ Henry VIII and his wives

➤ Francis Drake and the Spanish Armada

➤ Edward and the Wars of the Roses

➤ The great Plague

➤ The Fire of London

➤ Cromwell and the Civil War

➤ Florence Nightingale and the Crimean War

➤ Evacuees and the Second World War

➤ Otto Frank and the Holocaust

We already know from the story matrix that a good story needs two things for it to work: a character and an important problem to be solved. One way to create a good history story is to tell the story as biography, and then add the historical detail around that story. The story on page 129 of *Otto Frank* is a popular example of such a story, which can be used for exploring the Holocaust and WW2 for KS2/3. Another way is to take a general event and create a fictional character with a particular problem to illustrate what happened. *The Great Fire of London* story on page 130 is an example of this. It has been written for easy telling by KS1 classes. In both cases they can be mapped, stepped, spoken and deepened as a way into the topic.

For more history stories, see our forthcoming *History Stories for Primary School Children to Retell,* Storytelling Schools Series, Volume III, by Chris Smith and Adam Guillain.

Otto Frank

Once, in the country of Germany, in the city of Frankfurt, there was a man called Otto Frank. He was Jewish, meaning he followed a religion based on the Old Testament in the bible. As a teenager he fought for Germany in World War One, down in the trenches with his gun while bombs dropped and bullets whizzed around him killing many, but not him.

After the war he went home and married. Soon he had two children, Margot and Anne.

At this time the Nazis were getting strong in Germany. Hitler made speeches about Jews being bad and dirty and evil. Otto saw that soon things would be dangerous for the Jews so he moved his family to Amsterdam in Holland before it was too late.

When war broke out between Germany and other countries Otto saw that soon Amsterdam would be taken by the Germans so he applied for a visa to go to Cuba or USA, but before he could travel the Germans came.

Otto and his family hid in an attic in a house in Amsterdam, staying in hiding for two years, fearing for their lives, never going out. Then someone told the Germans that they were hiding there. One day a lorry full of soldiers surrounded the house and marched Otto and his family out at gunpoint. They were put on a train to Auschwitz in Poland, a work camp where Jews were forced to work like slaves, and when they were too sick to work they were put to death using poison gas.

Otto could not see his family in the camp, but somehow managed to live for six months. One day Russian troops freed everybody and told him the war was over. He travelled back to Amsterdam, looking for his wife and children but found nothing. Finally he accepted that they had died in the camps.

Then a friend gave him a pile of papers that he had found in the hideout. In them was the diary which Anne had written when she was in hiding, full of stories about what it was like being a child in hiding.

It was written in Dutch. Otto edited it and translated it into German and soon it became a famous book and play. Today the house where they hid has become a museum to help us remember the terrible things that happened in the war.

The Great Fire of London

Once, the city of London was built from houses of wood, with houses built so close together that there was just enough room to walk between them.

In the middle of London, close to the river, there was a bakery. The baker's son was called Jack. Jack didn't go to school. Instead he helped his dad in the shop.

Every day he'd start by chopping wood for the oven (*show chopping*)

Then he'd light the oven

Then he'd mix up the flour and water and yeast and knead the dough

Cut out the loaves

And bake them in the oven

One morning he woke up to the smell of burning. He jumped out of bed and ran down stairs. 'FIRE!' he shouted.

Someone had left the door of the oven open. A piece of burning wood must have jumped out of the door and set fire to wood shavings on the floor. There were flames everywhere.

He woke up his family and they rushed down to the river with buckets and ran back to the house. (In those days there were no taps, and no space for a wagon with water to move between the houses.)

By the time they got back the whole building was on fire. The water just hissed and fizzed into the flames.

The wind blew the fire to the next house down the street, and then the next, and then the next. Jack shouted, 'Wake up! Wake up!' and soon everyone was out in the street running to the river for water, but it spread too fast. Soon the bakery was just a pile of ash, and soon the whole street was gone as the fire spread in all directions.

The fire was travelling too fast to stop it with buckets of water, so the mayor made a plan. People knocked down houses in a circle around the fire so it could not spread any further. They worked with axes and saws, knocking down home after home, but the fire was too fast and caught them before they had finished.

In the end they brought gunpowder and blew up houses around the fire. Finally it was stopped. 200,000 people lost their homes in the fire. Jack and his dad went home and built a new home on the ruins of the old one and soon they were selling bread again.

Every day he'd start by chopping wood for the oven (*show chopping*)

Then he'd light the oven

Then he'd mix up the flour and water and yeast and knead the dough

Cut out the loaves

And bake them in the oven

But this time he was careful to make sure the oven door was always closed!

When they built new homes they made sure there were roads between them so water trucks could get to any fire, so the fire would not spread too far.

In addition it is worth remembering that you can use HMSS to remember any sequence. This is handy for revision skills, but also great for any history timeline. You may just want to map and step it and leave it at that. Opposite is an example of a timeline for Britain from prehistory to the present day. HMSS can be a great way to compress huge topics into something concise and manageable.

Mapping and stepping a history sequence: The history of the Britain

Item	Icon	Gesture
Dinosaurs		Roar with claws
Ice Age	Brrr	Shiver
Island		Tree and water
Hunter-gatherer		Archer pose
Farmer		Hoe digging
Villages		Roundhouse (mime its shape)
Iron		Sword (swing it)
Towns		Houses (mime roofs)
Industry		Machine (mime cogs and pistons)
Cities		Smoke (mime coughing)
Digital		Keyboard (mime typing)

Personal and Social Education (PSE)

Stories are great for introducing PSE themes for exploration and discussion. In *147 Traditional Stories for Primary School Children to Retell* (Hawthorn Press) all stories are indexed by theme so that you can look up suitable stories for whatever PSE theme you want to explore with your class. You can also search online story databases such as provided by the Story Museum.

Using stories allows you engage a class in an issue without telling them what to think, allowing them to draw their own conclusions. Give them a story and let them work out the learning and lessons: the learning part of the story matrix. You can also link this easily to the discussion function for non-fiction in various ways.

This section includes:

➤ Ways to use stories to explore a PSE theme

➤ Empathy

➤ Choice and consequences

➤ Discussion

Stories from one setting can also be reset in a modern context to explore contemporary relevance. Let's say you are exploring risks and consequences with your class. You might teach the class to tell the story of *Icarus* (page 134) using HMSS, and work in a number of ways:

➤ Discuss the learning in the story for father and son

➤ Discuss similar issues from real life

➤ Retell or re-enact the story and pause at places where a decision has been made and explore the options and consequences at those moments

➤ Find ways to reset the plot idea in a modern city or about a particular theme. Retell with new characters. Explore the options for tragedy and options for learning to make wise choices

➤ Identify interesting areas of enquiry for students to explore independently

➤ Create explanation and discussion pieces (oral or written) on the themes identified

Icarus

When Theseus killed the Minotaur, King Minos was furious. Theseus had killed his son and stolen the king's daughter away from right under his nose. Someone was to blame; someone had to pay; and that someone was Daedalus the smith, the man who had made the labyrinth.

Minos summoned Daedalus immediately.

'How can I help your majesty?' he smiled, confident as usual.

'All this is your fault!' snapped the king. 'You were told to build a maze so tangled that all who entered would never leave. Didn't you?'

'Yes, your majesty,' he argued, still calm. 'But you saw the thread; no maze can defeat a thread, however perfect.'

'I don't want excuses, and anyway I hear you were mixed up somehow with the queen in making that bull-headed child in the first place! What do you have to say about THAT?'

Daedalus hung his head.

'Nothing, your majesty. I only do what I am told to do. I cannot be responsible for what my superiors do with my creations...'

Minos shook his head. 'No blacksmith, you make them, you are responsible, and this time you will pay. You and your son can spend some time in my prison while I think what to do with you. Guards!'

Daedalus and Icarus were taken to the prison tower which the blacksmith himself had designed and built, and were locked inside the highest cell with a lock that Daedalus himself had made.

His son didn't like it there.

'Dad,' he whined, 'I want to go home.'

Daedalus patted the boy on his shoulder. 'Don't worry son, give me a week and I'll solve the problem.'

Every day Daedalus took half of the bread the guards gave them to eat, and scattered it on the windowsill of the cell.

Icarus was curious. 'Dad, what are you doing? I'm hungry.'

'Wait and see,' came the reply.

When the birds came to feed on the bread, Daedalus would crouch like a cat by the window and every now and then pounce on a bird, pull out its longest feathers, then let it go and wait for the next bird.

After a week he had a great pile of feathers.

In the evenings he saved half of the wax from the candles the guards gave them, and when he had saved enough he started working, sticking the feathers together with the wax, making two huge pairs of wings.

As ever, he was proud of his creation.

'Look son, these wings will take us away from here, to a new land with a new king to serve. But you have to be careful.'

'Don't worry, Dad!'

'No, LISTEN Icarus! This is important. The wings are made from wax and feathers. They are weak; you have to be careful. Fly straight and steady next to me and you'll be fine, but don't do anything else. Fly too high and the wax will melt in the sun's heat. Fly too low and the sea will wet the feathers and you will fall. Stay with me and we'll both be fine.'

'Don't worry Dad, I'll be alright.'

With the wings strapped to their arms and shoulders they stand, perched for a moment on the window ledge. Below them a bull bellows, above them an eagle hovers.

'Now!'

Together they fall into space, their wings catching the updraft of their falling. Their falling slows and then, meeting a pocket of rising air, they climb with it, above the tower, and glide, wingtip to wingtip, north over the cliffs, out over the ocean.

Icarus is delighted and excited.

'Look Dad! Look what I can see! Look down there, dolphins! This is great!'

'Just stay straight and steady.'

For some time they fly together, till Icarus grows restless.

'Dad, look what I can do!'

Icarus turns a somersault in mid-air.

'No son – it's dangerous. They aren't strong enough. Stay by me!'

'Dad, you worry too much. Look, watch me climb.'

Icarus begins to spiral up above his father, ignoring the pleas to return. He climbs higher and higher into the heat of the sun until he feels the drip of liquid wax on his shoulder and, in an instant, the feathers are gone. He plummets like a falling anvil, down past his father, smashing into the sea with such force that his spine snaps.

Daedalus hovers and watches his son's lifeless body floating in the water below, adding his own tears to the sea's stock of salt, as he feels, for the first time, the suffering which his own creations have caused.

Or let's say you want to look at the theme of death and bereavement. This might be explored through a great story like *Snip-snip*, which can be a powerful way to open a discussion about this subject.

Snip-snip

There was once a boy called Jack who loved his mum and dad but most of all loved his granddad. His granddad was a tailor. Jack loved to watch his granddad at work. On the day of Jack's fifth birthday he went to visit his granddad at his shop and Granddad gave him a wonderful new coat.

It fitted Jack like a glove. 'Thanks, Granddad,' he grinned. He ran out into the streets where he found his friends who all admired his new coat. 'My granddad made this for me. He's a tailor,' said Jack proudly. Jack loved his coat so much. He never took it off. He wore it here, he wore it there, he wore it everywhere – even over his pyjamas!

Time passed and Jack grew but of course the coat didn't. One day his mother said, 'That coat doesn't fit you anymore, Jack. It's splitting and frayed and beginning to smell. Let's throw it away and buy you a new one.' 'No,' said Jack. 'I love this coat.'

He took the coat to his granddad's shop. 'Don't worry,' said Granddad, 'I know what to do.'

Granddad took his scissors and began to cut away at the coat. As he did, he sang a little song.

> *Snip, snip, snip, this is what I do,*
> *Snipping here, snipping there, making something new.*
> *In and out and in, this is how I sew,*
> *Sewing things together, that's what I know.*

He sewed and he snipped, he snipped and he sewed, and when he was done, Jack saw that his Granddad had turned his coat into a beautiful new jacket. Jack put it on and it fitted him like a glove.

'Thanks, Granddad,' he grinned.

Jack loved his jacket so much. He never took it off. He wore it here, he wore it there, he wore it everywhere – even over his pyjamas.

Time passed and Jack grew but the jacket didn't. One day his mother said, 'That jacket doesn't fit you anymore, Jack. It's splitting and frayed and beginning to smell. Let's throw it away and buy you a new one.' 'No,' said Jack. 'I love this jacket!'

'Don't worry,' said Granddad, 'I know what to do.'

Granddad took his scissors and began to cut away at the jacket. As he did, he sang a little song.

> *Snip, snip, snip, this is what I do,*
> *Snipping here, snipping there, making something new.*
> *In and out and in, this is how I sew,*
> *Sewing things together, that's what I know.*

Jack's granddad turned Jack's jacket into a T-shirt. When the T shirt wore out he turned it into a little badge.

One day Jack looked down and the badge was gone.

He went to see his granddad. 'I've lost my badge. I loved it!' he wailed.

His granddad got out a piece of paper and pencil and wrote for a while, then handed the paper to Jack. It was this story, about Jack and the coat and the jacket and the T-shirt and the badge.

'Why have you given me this?' asked Jack.

His granddad smiled:

'Nothing in life lasts forever. In time everything gets lost or wears out: coats, jackets, T-shirts, badges. But, if you love something and you lose it, put it in a story and then every time you tell the story you will see the thing that you have lost. You see it in your imagination. Maybe that will help.'

Jack told the story to his friends, and he did feel better. He saw the things he had lost in his imagination as he told the story.

Later, when Jack's granddad died, Jack told this story at his funeral.

Empathy

Empathy is one of those things that matter a lot. Being able to imagine what others feel, to 'feel-with-them' (com-passion) is basic to successful human relating and social behaviour. Understanding the impact we have on the feelings of others helps us understand how to behave with others.

Storytelling is great for this. It's one thing to hear a story and passively imagine the action, but when you tell a story you have to really get into the shoes of the characters, finding them voices and gestures and understanding why they feel what they feel.

It's the same for storymaking. For a story to work we have to know what a character is thinking and feeling as the story goes on. The audience have to care about it. This is pure empathy in practice, a good example of Bruno Bettelheim's argument that stories provide a safe space for children to rehearse and master the world of feeling.

Sometimes you might also choose stories that model a particular feeling. For example, if you want to explore fear with the class you could tell the story of *Odysseus and the Cyclops*, and then talk about what the men felt when they were trapped in the cave.

You could then recycle the *Cyclops* plot into a modern familiar setting like the students' own community and explore other dangers and fears that might be experienced. This could be done using the story matrix, with a focus on a problem involving danger and fear.

Choosing

There are loads of ways to explore wise and unwise choices using stories. One way is to work from a learned story using the Icarus example on page 134. Generally you can tell a tragedy and then discuss what might happen if other choices were made. Tragedies are great for this as they usually have a fatal character flaw that leads to continued unwise choices, or a lesson that the character fails to learn. You may then retell the story and invite the class to think of wiser choices that might be made and the consequences. For example, Macbeth might negotiate a power sharing arrangement, Little Red Riding Hood might pay more attention to whom she is talking to, the Little Red Hen might find a way to get help earlier, and so on. You can also pause the story at the dilemma/choice moment and have the class complete it with various choice options both wise and unwise. What if the prince loses patience with Cinderella always running away, and locks her in the tower!

Discussions

The discussion function for non-fiction can be used extensively to explore PSE themes arising from such stories, from various sides of the story. For example:

➤ Should the wolf be punished?

➤ Was it right to kill the giant?

➤ How might Cinderella deal with her stepsisters?

You may also link such discussions to everyday life. If you were in a similar situation, what would you think, feel and do?

Thinking-feeling-choosing

This triad is used in psychology to understand human behaviour and experience. Each element is important for daily life:

> ➤ Do we understand and feel understood?

> ➤ Can we relate to the feelings of others and ourselves?

> ➤ Are we able to choose and allow others to choose freely?

We can rehearse these three elements in storytelling and storymaking. You can always ask the class the three questions:

> ➤ What is the character thinking?

> ➤ What is the character feeling?

> ➤ What choices might the character make?

Answering these questions will help make a story that is more satisfying to tell and hear, while enabling rehearsal of three core skills that, if learned, will serve us well in daily life.

Truth and story

Some might say that stories have evolved with humans to help teach positive values to us all. In PSE you can use them in this way. Here's a story about that.

Once, when the world was new, Truth went about telling everyone all about their own shortcomings and what they should do about it. Everyone else found this annoying, especially as Truth was always right. Soon Truth had no friends and no one would listen to her. She noticed someone else going around who was very popular. This friendly old woman would sit and tell tales about this and that. People loved to listen and talk together about the stories afterwards. Truth noticed that people talked quite happily about things that were wrong and what needed doing, just using ideas from the story.

That's why Truth became a storyteller.

Religion

All religions are rich in the stories which carry their message. You can tell them and teach them to your class as an engaging way to explore a particular religion. The lives of the founders and main teachers and the stories that they tell are full of great material.

As these stories are, for some, sacred stories, it's usually better to stick with the original rather than innovating and changing the plots, as for some this might seem disrespectful. It's usually fine teaching telling and deepening then linking to

discussions of themes and learnings in the story. Storytelling will bring all this alive whatever the faith and non-faith mix of your class.

Here's a great little communal nativity story, which was developed with St John Fisher School in Oxford. They developed it in the Foundation stage and then taught it to the whole school during their Christmas assembly with a full set of actions to go with the words. It was full of joy and fun, while remaining respectful and true to the spirit of the Christmas celebration.

Nativity Chant

A long long time ago
Mary was going to have a baby
They walked and walked and walked and walked
And slept in a stable

SNOW IS FALLING
STARS ARE SHINING
HALLELUYA BABY JESUS

In the cold of the dark dark night
When everyone was sleeping
Jesus was born to Mary
And lay in the straw of a manger

SNOW IS FALLING
STARS ARE SHINING
HALLELUYA BABY JESUS

Who's that knocking at the stable door?
LOOK it's the shepherds
What will they give to baby Jesus?
Sheepskins and wool

SNOW IS FALLING
STARS ARE SHINING
HALLELUYA BABY JESUS

Who's that knocking at the stable door?
LOOK it's the three wise men
What will they give to baby Jesus?
Gold, frankincense and myrrh

SNOW IS FALLING
STARS ARE SHINING
HALLELUYA BABY JESUS

Who's that knocking at the stable door?
WE ARE, WE ARE
What will we learn from baby Jesus?
Joy, love and hope

SNOW IS FALLING
STARS ARE SHINING
HALLELUYA BABY JESUS

Science

There are various ways to integrate storytelling into your science topics.

One simple way is to use a biography story of a scientist to introduce a topic and the way that a new discovery was made. An example could be Benjamin Franklin discovering electricity with his kite. You can first teach the class to tell the story, explore the scientific questions it raises, then connect these questions to the main theme.

Benjamin Franklin's Kite

Once there was an American scientist called Benjamin Franklin. In 1752 he was studying lightning. He knew that when you rub together certain materials they would stick together by some unknown force, and that same force could make your hair stand on end. Sometimes when the force was very strong you could see sparks moving between the two objects.

Franklin wondered whether the fire of the lightning was made out of the same stuff as the sparks from 'charged' objects. He decided to put a metal rod on top of his house connected to a wire, to see if he could collect some of the lightning when it struck the rod. But before the rod was built a thunderstorm came over his house. Thinking quickly he thought of flying a kite up into the thundercloud to see if he could collect any lightning that way.

He took a piece of silk, two sticks and a ball of thread wound around a piece of metal, and made a kite which he flew up into the cloud on the fierce wind.

He stood in the pouring rain and waited, his feet wet and his teeth chattering.

For a while nothing happened, and then he noticed that frayed pieces of wet string on the kite line were standing up in the air individually as if repelling on another, just as if they had been close to a charged object.

When he touched the metal at the bottom of the string he saw sparks jump between metal and hand. He thought this showed that lightning and the 'charged' objects were carrying the same stuff, although it was a long time before scientists found out what that stuff, electricity, was made of.

Later he built the rod on his roof and connected it by wires to a bell. Whenever lightning struck the rod, something moved down the wire and caused the bell to ring.

This thing became known as electricity.

Another option is to take a story and discuss the scientific content. Let's say you are teaching forces to infants in a class. You might first teach them *The Giant Turnip* and then role-play the pulling and resistance of the turnip before introducing the idea of forces and resistance. Or let's say you are teaching plant growth to infants: you could teach them the *Little Red Hen* and then explore the process of growth from seed to mature wheat.

Also, science is full of important sequences that need to be learned in the right order and which can be challenging to learn. For this you can use 'map, step, speak' to learn and remember them. It's quick, easy and effective. See the box below for an example of teaching the digestion sequence in humans.

Then you can use the various non-fiction types to present discussions, explanations and reports about the content of the topic.

Stage	Icon		Gesture
Hand	Hand		Putting food in the mouth
Mouth	Mouth		Chewing
Swallowing	Neck		Swallowing
Stomach: digestion	Stomach		Point to belly and say, 'digestion'
Small Intestine	Small Intestine		Point and say, 'absorption of nutrients'
Large Intestine	Large Intestine		Point and say, 'absorption of water'
Excretion	Toilet		Sitting on the loo

Music

Just as with poetry, there are loads of ways to integrate music teaching with storymaking. Music brings a new dimension to a story, creating mood, variety and engagement. All stories can be turned into songs and songs can always be added into stories. Music can be used before a story, between story sections, and at the end. It can be huge fun to sometimes think of popular songs that might be used as part of a story performance, making it a kind of musical. This can generate huge enthusiasm.

Here's a checklist of options to consider:

➤ Compose a song story with the class and then let students compose their own

➤ Compose a song that a character or narrator might sing

➤ Retell the story using only music and sound

➤ Listen to a piece of instrumental music as a stimulus for storymaking

➤ Listen to a song as a stimulus for story-making

➤ Step the story with a song for each step

➤ Choose or compose a piece of music to play before, during or after a storytelling

➤ Create a dance movement for each step in the story and link them together with music for a dance retelling

➤ Perform the whole story as an improvised opera

➤ Create a musical of the story

➤ Explore rhythm by telling over a drum or sound pulse

➤ Explore the use of sound to create mood

How to compose a quick song for a story

➤ Brainstorm words for a song

➤ Choose a simple song (*twinkle twinkle, baa baa black sheep*, etc.)

➤ Fit new words to the tune. Keep singing and improvising till it works

➤ Find a new tune for the new words

➤ Demonstrate this as shared composing, then try in pairs and small groups

Chapter 11

Making it happen

Becoming a Storytelling School

In this final chapter we look at how to adopt the storytelling model in your school. We cover some of the main issues that schools have highlighted during adoption of the approach, such as:

➤ School leadership

➤ Launching the policy

➤ Building up skills step by step

➤ Including teaching support staff

➤ Including parents

➤ Celebration and visibility

➤ Whole school planning

➤ Using support networks

We have worked with many schools who have successfully adopted the Storytelling Schools model and also with a good number who have tried adoption and not succeeded. In this final section we describe what we have learned from these experiences.

Diversity is the spice of life

Every school is different and there is no single model for how to adopt a storytelling approach. Some schools plan centrally and issue quite detailed instructions. Some schools offer general guidelines and leave details up to the individual teachers. Some schools do a lot of up-front training and then adopt the whole package of telling, deepening, shared writing and non-fiction in one go. Others introduce the scheme gradually over several years. All of these approaches can be worked well: we are not saying that there is just one way to become a Storytelling School, but there are some general principles to think about when making plans. Some schools set the policy in motion in advance, others let it evolve. Here are some basic tips:

➤ Initially, it is good to stimulate interest, excitement and a shared vision about becoming a Storytelling School in teachers, students and parents. This generates the willingness to adopt new methods and explore new ideas.

➤ It is best to plan in advance the resources (stories, story curriculum) and training needed to create storytelling classrooms. This may be needed over several years and must include the induction of new staff.

➤ There needs to be someone in charge of monitoring and feedback, so that good practice can be shared, less confident teachers can be supported and impacts on students' learning can be assessed.

➤ Over time, various aspects of the overall scheme can be introduced until the whole approach is embedded and refined.

➤ School 'policy' may be set up-front or evolve through this experience. What works for your staff and students is what counts.

School leadership

The head teacher is of course crucial for leading and managing any school change, so a firm decision to become a Storytelling School on the part of the head and senior school management is an essential first step. This may sound obvious but it can be an issue. Becoming a Storytelling School means restructuring how learning happens in every classroom in the school.

Once the new policy has been agreed by the governors, senior management has to lead the way by introducing staff to the new approach. Various kinds of support will be needed so that storytelling can be established. A demonstration of storytelling approaches from senior staff to others can be very helpful, whether in school assemblies, staff meetings or in the classroom. It is also crucial that staff are both persuaded and inspired by the idea: this process can be supported in part by external consultants or by visiting other schools, but senior management need to be persuaded and inspired too, and communicate that spirit to the rest of the school.

Of course, there has to be an action plan. It is not enough to pay for a school training day and then expect a Storytelling School to materialise: there are issues relating to resources, time, curriculum, assessment and support that need to be put in place and adapted as the changes proceed. Some schools we have worked with have sent a couple of teachers for a day's training, asked them to run a staff inset and then hoped the ideas would trickle down into classroom teaching practice. This may work to provide some teachers in a school with some new skills for teaching language, but this will not lead by itself to the whole school restructuring its learning.

Schools often suffer from a stream of new initiatives and requirements from government and elsewhere, adding complication and confusion to the lives of staff. If the Storytelling School concept is experienced as another annoying initiative it is unlikely to succeed. For the head teacher, the key is to make a decision and announce it, then delegate the planning details to a senior staff member, usually the deputy head or literacy coordinator. This level of delegation in itself sends out a strong message about the importance given to the policy.

Launching the initial policy

Ideally when the initial policy is launched staff will feel:

> Convinced that it will work with their students.

> Confident that they will be able to teach in this way.

> Clear about what they are expected to do.

> Reassured that they would get the support they need.

Different schools will do this in different ways. In some, a decision is made by senior management, a set of stories for the year linked to curriculum is selected, and then at a whole school inset an announcement is made, more or less, that this is what the school is going to do. This approach can work well for some schools. Other schools prefer a process of consultation and discussion with staff before a final decision and plan is made. This can involve some taster trainings and consultation on story curriculum with the staff.

Whatever the lead up to the launch, the event itself has to be a great experience: usually it will consist of a one-day training at the beginning of a term where the staff learn to tell stories and teach their students to do the same (i.e. covering the material in the first two chapters of this handbook). We have found that doing this well is probably the most important part of the process. If staff go away having had a good time, having enjoyed playing and connecting with stories, and feel ready to have a go with teaching storytelling in their classroom, the approach has a good chance of succeeding. It is usually critical that teachers actually go through the process of learning and telling stories themselves in the training, so that they can experience the fun of it and overcome any nervous resistance. If they are able to tell a story during training, it will be far easier to tell it in their classroom.

Make sure the launch is run with a trainer who knows how to inspire and energise a group using active learning by doing. This is not about PowerPoints and schemes: it is all about having a great day. After these sessions many teachers say they are reminded of why they became teachers and of the way they would love to teach. Often there is a 'Wow!' moment when the penny drops and the ideas just fall into place.

Also the stories need to be available for the teachers to start telling straightaway so that they can go into their classrooms the next day and start, with the memory of the training still clear in their minds. Launch trainings should include a few stories that all the teachers can go and teach to their classes the next day: *The Freedom Song, Monkeys and Hats, Honey and Trouble* are three good starters. There should then be a story linked to the curriculum that the class will work on that term, ideally available on audio.

Usually that's enough to begin with – the first step of getting your teachers telling stories and teaching their classes to tell. Whoever is coordinating the change needs to be in touch with teachers during the first few weeks, helping them iron out difficulties.

Building up the skills step by step

In order to become a Storytelling School your teachers will need to develop their set of teaching skills: for some, many of the things in this handbook will be familiar and they may simply need some support to integrate and adjust their teaching. For others much of it will be completely new, challenging and perhaps daunting. Most schools will have teachers in both categories.

This usually works best with a series of training sessions over the following year or two, run by either external trainers, in-school staff, or teachers from other schools, to include:

➤ Teaching students to retell a story

➤ Deepening

➤ Shared writing

➤ Innovation

➤ Invention

➤ Non-fiction

➤ Curriculum links

For some schools, deepening and shared writing will be a priority because they give the teachers an immediate repertoire of things to do with the story once it has been told, and show how to make the all-important link to writing improvement. In most cases, it is better for teachers to learn these activities by doing them in the training scheme before trying them out and adapting them in their classrooms. Spread over one or more years, a staff development programme might look like this:

1. Overview and how to teach children to retell stories.

2. How to deepen children's understanding and engagement in a story.

3. Shared writing – from telling into writing by innovating.

4. Inventing new stories.

5. Teaching non-fiction.

Each training session needs to be followed with the expectation that everyone will try out the activities. This can be planned out in the school's curriculum map.

Including teaching support staff

Try to get support staff involved in the storytelling from the beginning, either during the initial training or in a bespoke training session. This will have a number of benefits.

Benefits of including support staff

✓ Some support staff will be excellent storytellers. It does not always have to be the teacher who tells and teaches the story. If teaching assistants are given time to prepare their stories, they will not feel that too much is being asked of them.

✓ Many support staff have been members of the school community for longer than the teachers or head teachers. Building their storytelling skills is therefore more sustainable for the school.

✓ Many teaching support staff are part of the local community: their voices will tell and retell stories in cultural styles that the students are used to, often with distinctive modes of humour, idioms and local references. Support staff may engage with stories in a way that is not possible for teachers.

✓ Students in the storytelling classroom do a lot of work with small groups and individuals as they create their stories. Support staff may have the job of mentoring and helping during these sessions. If they have learned how to tell, deepen, innovate and write stories, they will be able to coach students through that same process.

Parents

Parents get involved in storytelling by listening to their children telling stories. This can be simply by having homework sessions where the student takes home a story map plus a request that someone at home listens to the child telling the story from the map. It can be a map the student has drawn or a standard story map. In some schools, a feedback sheet went out to parents about what they liked when listening to the story: many classes achieved a response rate of nearly 100 per cent. Students may retell the story at home in their mother tongue if needed. Some of the story games like 'Tell me more' and 'Fortunately/Unfortunately' can also go home for story practice.

Some schools feel the need to explain to parents why storytelling is important for education, and how it works, as perceptions of education vary so widely. This can be in book bag notes, during storytelling sessions at the end of the day to which parents are invited, in the school newsletter, on the school website or in other school events where parents gather together.

Celebration and visibility

In a Storytelling School there can be lots of opportunities for celebration and affirmation of the work of classes, for both teachers and students. Here are some ways of providing these:

Whole school stories

Some schools choose a whole school story at the beginning of the year and everyone works on it exclusively for a few weeks. Often, the school is decorated with the various landscapes of the story and, as each class creates work, it is exhibited around the school. In some schools, adults dress up as characters from the story, appear at unexpected times and then disappear again. For example, on one occasion a wolf rode through the school hall during assembly on a unicycle. This kind of activity generates a huge amount of excitement and enthusiasm for the overall project.

In order to continue with a story for a few weeks, teachers have to know how to link a told story to deepening, innovation, topic work and writing. Stories can be enhanced by artwork, model making, puppet work, music, song, dance, cartoon and filmmaking.

Storytelling assemblies

There are various ways for class stories to be celebrated during school assembly:

➤ A few students tell the story to the school, each taking a section of the story.

➤ The rest of the class participate in a re-enactment on stage while the story is being told.

➤ A 'show and tell' session can honour the various storytelling achievements of students within the class.

Classroom and corridor displays

Selected story creations can be displayed on the classroom wall and in school corridors for the school community to admire.

Storytelling between classes

Some stories can be learned with the purpose of telling them to younger classes in the school. For example KS2 pupils might learn and rehearse a story then visit another class. One format is for two storytellers to sit with two or three listeners as they hear the story being told. This gives a sense of purpose for learning and retelling the story.

Planning stories into the curriculum

Many storytelling schools start off by planning six stories per year, per class, which will be learned, retold and worked with over several weeks in the way described in this handbook. Often these stories are matched up to topics as shown in Chapter 10 (p. 117). This is probably a good place to start with planning. The task of

learning six stories, specially selected for the topics and provided to teachers, should not be too daunting. Each student would then learn a minimum of about 40 stories from Foundation to Year 6. The whole school needs to be involved in the process to avoid different classes choosing the same story.

After that, most schools focus on planning in more detail the ways that the chosen stories can support the learning of particular language features every year. Again the language features need to be a whole school policy otherwise there may be duplication or omission. Some schools also link their non-fiction literacy planning into the scheme.

Finally, many schools broaden their use of the storytelling method to cover topics in history, geography, religious education and science. In all cases, it is a matter of identifying a narrative within the subject area that can be retold in an enjoyable way. Some schools develop their own stories for this. Others seek help from consultants and advisers to identify and sometimes write suitable narratives.

Induction of new staff

A few schools experience high turnover of teaching staff, especially in the most challenging teaching environments. This means that every year new teachers will have to receive some induction into the storytelling method. You could do this during staff meetings where new teachers are shown by existing staff how the scheme works. Some identify a staff member to provide this induction, while others use external trainers. New teachers find having a 'Story Buddy' very helpful and appreciate observing other teachers working on the different stages.

Support networks

Occasionally, a partnership of primary schools decides to adopt the Storytelling School model together, sharing some of the costs of training, accessing partnership funding, and providing opportunities for schools to support one another in many ways. One way this can happen is to create a support group of storytelling coordinators who meet a few times a year to share experiences and ideas as well as supporting each other's work.

Another way is for the staff that are most experienced in storytelling to visit schools that want help to demonstrate classroom technique to those who need it. Conversely, staff can visit other schools to observe teaching and learn in that way. Learning from colleagues in a non-threatening atmosphere can be very powerful.

Falling in love with a story

The Storytelling School model works well because it is fun. Because it is fun, teachers and students feel fulfilled and enjoy learning and retelling their stories, whether spoken or written. This pleasure is driven by a love of stories.

Keep this in mind in leading your Storytelling School. Find stories that you and your staff love and your teachers will pass that love on to their students. In some ways it's as simple as that. Find the right stories for your school and help everyone remember to enjoy them. That's the key to becoming a dynamic Storytelling School. It's all about the magic.

Afterword

So now you know: you've read about telling the story, teaching your class to retell it, you've got a toolbox of warm-ups and you know about deepening, innovation, invention, and shared writing. You also know how to link stories to language and subject learning. With the plot matrix as your guide and the basic plots as your helpers, you have everything you need to start becoming a Storytelling School. We hope you enjoy the journey. There will be obstacles and setbacks but with the right helpers and qualities we predict a happy beginning, middle and ending. Good luck. These stories have been told for sometimes hundreds and sometimes thousands of years. They are part of our human heritage, helping us develop in many varied and wonderful ways. May they touch the hearts and minds of your staff, students and their families!

Another story to help you on your way follows on page 152. It is a great story to start with. You can listen to it on the Story Museum website: **www.storymuseum.org.uk/1001stories**

Typical steps to becoming a Storytelling School

➤ School gets to know the idea.

➤ Head teacher decides to become a Storytelling School with a minimum of six stories per year storytelling curriculum and defined relationships to literacy and/or topic teaching.

➤ Head teacher decides on lead staff member for storytelling and defines relationship with literacy planning, cross-curricular planning and drama.

➤ Create and collect resources of story texts, audios and teaching tools.

➤ Finalise lead stories, consult and launch with staff together with training on warm-ups, how to tell and teach your class to tell, and story deepening (Chapters 1–5). Ensure that teachers are persuaded of the approach. Monitor and assess and support.

➤ Ensure that all staff have skills to teach writing using shared writing (Chapter 8) techniques or similar so that language richness can flow through to writing. Provide training then monitor, assess and support.

➤ Consider setting up a language and narrative progression policy for the school (Chapter 10) and ensure that all staff understand it and are able to teach the necessary language features using their stories, both in storytelling and in writing stages. (This may include whole school agreed actions for key language features.)

There is the possibility to integrate specific plot types and progression/coverage of this across the stories, with specific teaching of plot types/character functions.

➤ Set up a non-fiction policy for the school (Chapter 9), sometimes linking to the fiction story, and make sure that teachers understand and are able to teach with storytelling and shared writing. Monitor, assess and support. Consider a language progression policy for non-fiction texts.

➤ Define ways to integrate the storytelling methods into the teaching of other topics in the curriculum.

➤ Ensure that all teachers are familiar with the relevant skills for innovation and invention in storytelling and story writing.

➤ Plan for annual induction of new staff: resource pack, in/out house training, and support.

➤ Plan for active inclusion of all teaching staff in the storytelling classroom.

➤ Define relationships to professional development, staff supervision and evaluation. Create routine reporting system so that literacy coordinator can keep track of what is happening and respond.

➤ Review school environment – how can classroom and corridors reflect, support and inspire. Pictures, murals, words, messages, school website.

➤ Develop links with parents: storymaps home, newsletter, story collection, local stories and so on.

Monkeys and Hats

Once, not twice, not thrice ...

But once, there was a hat-maker. He made tall hats and short hats, fat hats and thin hats, green hats and blue hats ... all sorts of hats.

One day he was walking through the forest on the way to market, carrying a basketful of hats on his head to sell in the market. As he walked he sang a song.

'I am going to market, to market, to market,
I am going to market, to sell my hats.'

It was hot day and the hat-maker felt tired so he decided to have a rest. He lay down under a tree with his basket of hats next to him and fell asleep.

When he woke up, he looked in the basket and ... all the hats were gone. He looked behind trees and under bushes but there was no sign of his hats.

Then he heard the sound of a monkey chattering above his head. He looked up and saw, sitting on a branch high up above his head, a crowd of monkeys, each one wearing one of his hats.

Furious, he shook his fist at them and shouted: 'Give me back my hats!'

Now monkeys love to copy and all of the monkeys did the same thing back to him, shaking their fists and shouting back in monkey-talk.

This made the hat-maker even more cross. He shook his finger at the monkeys: 'If you are making fun of me then you'll be sorry!'

The monkeys copied him, wagged their fingers and shouted back in their own language.

'If you don't give them back, then I'll go and get my bow and arrow and shoot you one by one!'

He made as if to shoot an imaginary weapon and the monkeys just followed suit.

'Please,' he begged, his hands clasped together in prayer, but again they just copied.

This went on for a while, until finally he gave up and, taking off his own hat he threw it onto the ground. 'I give up!' he shouted.

All the monkeys in their trees took off their hats and threw them down onto the ground. Delighted, the hat-maker picked them up, put them in his basket, and walked off to town singing his song.

That evening the hat-maker told his son what had happened with the monkeys, and after that the monkey story was his son's favourite.

'Tell me, Dad! Tell me the one about the monkeys and the hats!'

The son grew up and became a hat-maker like his dad. One day he was walking through the forest with a basketful of hats, singing a song. He decided to have a rest. He lay down under a tree and fell asleep, and when he woke up ... his basket was empty.

Knowingly, he looked up into the tree and smiled at the monkeys wearing his hats.

He waggled his finger at them. 'I know how to get the hats back,' he called up, and the monkey waggled their fingers back to him.

He poked his chest confidently. 'My dad told me this story!' and again they copied, poking their chests.

He took off his hat, and threw it down, but the monkeys didn't move a muscle.

He waited. Nothing happened.

'Come on, you stupid monkeys!' he called, 'copy that!' but they didn't.

The largest of the monkeys, grey and long-haired, hung his hat on the branch and climbed down the tree until he stood face to face with the hat-maker's son.

'You think you are clever,' said the big monkey waggling his finger at the hat-maker's son, 'because your dad told you stories. Well, our dads told us stories too, and this time we're keeping the hats!'

The monkeys disappeared into the forest with the hats.

The hat-maker's son went home with nothing to sell in the market.

That's why stories are so important. You never know what you will learn from one, and when it will come in handy!

When you give it
away, you keep it.

It moves from place
to place and changes
as it moves.

Without it there is no past
or future, no reason
or meaning.

What is it?

A STORY!

Sources and resources

Here we credit the main sources that inspired the retellings in this book, and also provide examples of web and print resources associated with these tales that you might want to use in the classroom.

The Three Dolls

Most versions of this tale use a king as the main protagonist. I have chosen to reset the tale in a school to illustrate the relevance of its message to the Storytelling School's model for education. It sums up the value of storytelling so well!

I first read a version by David Novak in *Ready-to-Tell Tales,* edited by Holt and Mooney (August House, Atlanta, 1995), who reports first hearing it from an Indian storyteller Mr. Dasgupta. There is another retelling by David Heathfield reportedly from Persia on the World Stories website. www.worldstories.org.uk/stories/story/36-the-three-dolls

The story is used by the Hindu Guru, Bhagavân S'rî Sathya Sai Baba, as a spiritual teaching story. You can read this version online at www.askbaba.helloyou.ch/stories/s1004.html or find it in his teaching book, *Chinna Katta.*

Morgan Schatz Blackrose retells the story on her site www.morganschatzblackrose.wordpress.com/2013/05/01/the-three-dolls/ citing Novak's version and also another Indian variant called *The Three Statues.*

There is a delightful clip of children in a Punjabi school re-enacting the story in English on: www.youtube.com/watch?v=Y6gapQG8_fg called *The Secret of the Three Dolls.*

You can also find another storyteller telling the story on the *Times Education Supplement* website: www.tes.co.uk/teaching-resource/The-Three-Dolls-A-Story-about-Storytelling-6316374/ with tips on how to use it to teach speaking and listening. www.highlightskids.com/Stories/Fiction/F0299_threestatues.asp

The Freedom Song

This story was brought to the West by David Holt (see *Freedom Bird* in his *Ready-to-Tell Tales,* August House, Atlanta, 1995), who reports being told it in Thailand by his guide during a trip there.

There is another valuable version by Bill Harley with notes on techniques for participative telling in *Joining In,* edited by Teresa Miller (Yellow Moon Press, 1988).

You can also listen to Joanie Stewart tell the story on YouTube: www.youtube.com/watch?v=IjgOGLjtKGM

There is also an audio version on the Storytelling School website: www.storytellingschools.com.

It is a fantastic story full of play and wit. Thanks for finding it, David!

Anansi and the Tiger

This is another much loved and much told story, from the Caribbean. I first heard it told by Jan Blake and then by TUUP. You can hear it told at the Story Museum website (storymuseum.org.uk/1001stories). You can also find it in any number of Anansi collections.

There is a picture book version by Jennifer Bent called *How Anansi Captured the Tiger Stories: A Folk Tale from the Caribbean* (Dutton, 1996)

Snip-Snip

This is our retelling of a very popular Jewish tradition folktale. I first heard it from Adele Moss and then from the wonderful David Bash. It is a favourite of many storytellers around the world.

You can also hear Hugh Lupton tell an early years version in the excellent *The Story Tree* CD (Barefoot Books, 2001).

You can see Jenni Cargill-Strong telling her version on YouTube and check out the text on her website:

www.storytree.com.au/the-blue-coat-a-jewish-folktale-inspired-by-a-retelling-by-hugh-lupton/

Another telling by Maureen Wagner can be seen at www.strongstart.blogspot.co.uk/2010/12/story-blue-coat.htm

You can find our audio version at the Storytelling Schools website and also on the Story Museum website (storymuseum.org.uk/1001stories)

Monkeys and Hats

This is in many, many storytellers' repertoires and as you can see below is claimed as both an Indian and African folktale. In my retelling, as usual, I try to emphasise the way that storytelling is validated by the tale. There are loads of written storybook versions around, sometimes called *Monkey See, Monkey Do*. I can't remember where I first heard it: it never ceases to be wonderful!

Here are a few sources:
Monkey See, Monkey Do, Blue level 2 (Reading Corner) by Anne Adeney and Christina Bretschneider (Franklin Watts, 2006).

The Hat Maker and the Chimps, Collins Big Cat Phonics, Blue/Band 4, Adam Guillain and Cristian Bernadini (Collins, 2011).

The Hatseller And The Monkeys (African Version) Baba Wague Diakite (Scholastic Press, New York, 2000).

You can hear our version retold on the Story Museum website:
www.storymuseum.org.uk/1001stories

Icarus

Retellings of the Icarus myth can be found in most collections of ancient Greek myths. One early version is in Ovid's *Metamorphoses*, and I am very fond of the Ted Hughes version in his *Tales from Ovid* (Faber and Faber, 1997). For an informed source I always go first to the definitive *Greek Myths* by Robert Graves (Penguin Books, 1995).

Here is a picture book for early years:
Icarus, the Boy Who Could Fly, First Greek Myths by Saviour Pirotta and Jan Lewis (Orchard Books, 2006).

Here are a few good collections for children to start with:

Greek Myths by Marcia Williams (Walker Books, 1991).

The Usborne Book of Greek Myths, Usborne Myths & Legends by Anna Milbourne, Louie Stowell, Elena Temporin and Simona Bursi (Usborne Publishing Ltd, 2010).

The Orchard Book of Greek Myths by Geraldine McCaughrean and Emma Chichester Clark (Orchard Books, 1992).

D'Aulaire's Book of Greek Myths by Ingri D'Aulaire and Edgar Parin D'Aulaire (Delacorte Press, imprint of Random House Inc., New York, 1962).

If you ever get the chance to hear the *Metamorphoses* show of Hugh Lupton and Daniel Morden, it is brilliant top telling, including a fabulous *Icarus*.

Further reading

Story collections

Published by Barefoot Books

Story Time: First Tales for Sharing (book and CD). Retold by Stella Blackstone, illustrated by Anne Wilson. CD narrated by Jim Broadbent (this edition, 2008). Ages 3 to 7

Tales of Wisdom and Wonder (book and CD). Retold by Hugh Lupton and Niamh Sharkey (2006)

The Adventures of Odysseus. Retold by Daniel Morden and Hugh Lupton, illustrated by Christina Balit (2006). Ages 8 and up

The Barefoot Book of Animal Tales. Retold by Naomi Adler, illustrated by Amanda Hall (paperback, 2006). Ages 5 to 11

The Story Tree: Tales to Read Aloud (book and CD). Retold by Hugh Lupton, illustrated by Sophie Fatus (paperback edition, 2004)

And many more.

Retold by Geraldine McCaughrean

Britannia: 100 Great Stories From British History. Illustrated by Richard Brassey (Orion Children's, 2004)

100 World Myths and Legends. Illustrated by Bee Willey (Dolphin paperback, out of print)

Orchard Book of Greek Myths. Illustrated by Emma Chichester Clark (Orchard, 1992)

Orchard Book of Roman Myths. Illustrated by Emma Chichester Clark (Orchard, 2003)

Collected by David Holt

Ready-to-Tell Tales: From around the World. (American Storytelling) edited by David Holt and Bill Mooney (August House, 1995)

More Ready-to-Tell Tales: From around the World. Edited by David Holt and Bill Mooney (August House, 2000)

Other collections

Atticus the Storyteller: 100 Stories from Greece. Retold by Lucy Coats, illustrated by Antony Lewis (Orion Children's, new edition 2003)

Our Island Story: A History of Britain for Boys and Girls, from the Romans to Queen Victoria. H.E. Marshall (Galore Park Publishing, 2005)

Egyptian Myths. Jacqueline Morley, illustrated by Giovanni Caselli (Hodder Wayland, 2001, currently out of print)

The Extraordinary Coincidence of Stories Told in All Times, in All Places. Collected by Idries Shah (Octagon Press, 1991). Age 10 plus

The Singing Sack: 28 Song-stories from around the World (book and CD). Retold by Helen East, edited by Sheena Roberts, illustrated by Mary Currie (A & C Black, new edition 2000)

Three Rapping Rats: Making Music with Traditional Stories. Retold by Kaye Umansky, edited by Ana Sanderson, illustrated by Dee Shulman (A&C Black Musicals, 2004)

Background reading

The Seven Basic Plots: Why We Tell Stories
Christopher Booker (Continuum International
Publishing Group, 2005)

By Pie Corbett

*The Bumper Book of Storytelling into Writing: Key
Stage 1* (Clown Publishing, 2006)

*The Bumper Book of Storytelling into Writing: Key
Stage 2* (Clown Publishing, 2007)

*Jumpstart! Storymaking Games and Activities for
ages 7 to 12* (David Fulton Books, 2008)

*Talk for Writing across the Curriculum: How to
teach non-fiction writing 5–12 years* with Julia
Strong (Oxford University Press, 2007)

Writing Models. Individual titles for Years 3, 4, 5, 6
(David Fulton Books, 2005)

And many more.

Games, workshop models and literacy links

Earthtales, Storytelling in Times of Change. Alida
Gersie (The Merlin Press, London, 1992, out of
print)

Storymaking in Education and Therapy.
Alida Gersie and Nancy R. King (Jessica Kingsley
Publishing, 1989)

*Storytelling Games: Creative Activities for
Language, Communication, and Composition
Across the Curriculum.* Doug Lipman (Oryx Press,
1994, out of print)

Storytelling Schools Series

At Storytelling Schools we are passionate about the power of storytelling to transform education and learning. When storytelling skills are systematically taught throughout the school, students can use the approach to build confidence and fluency in spoken language, and to raise standards of reading and writing. Storytelling also provides an engaging, inclusive and enjoyable approach to subjects across the curriculum. At Storytelling Schools we offer information, resources and training to teachers who wish to adopt this approach in their school. Hawthorn Press will publish the Storytelling Schools Series over the next two years in partnership with Storytelling Schools.

Please check **www.hawthornpress.com** for book publication dates. To order books in advance, please email **orders@booksource.net** or telephone (0845) 3700063.

Available Spring 2014

147 Traditional Stories for Primary School Children to Retell
Storytelling Schools Series, Volume II
Chris Smith

This amazing resource is your one-stop-shop for inspirational primary school storytelling (age 5–11). This unique collection of tried-and-tested stories has a comprehensive set of indexes classifying the stories by age suitability, related topic, values, genre, plot type and country of origin, for easy reference and story selection.

The volume was created to help storytelling schools to plan their own story curriculum. However, it will be of interest and value to any primary school teacher wishing to incorporate oral storytelling into their teaching. Together with the companion volume, *The Storytelling School Handbook for Teachers*, it provides an

essential reference for any school wishing to adopt the Storytelling School approach.

'I have been collecting stories matched up to common primary topics for the past ten years. These stories have all been told by me and then used by teachers. We know the stories work well, engage and inspire children. The collection is a simple one-stop-shop for primary school storytelling, allowing quick access and topic links. It takes ages otherwise to find the right story and work out whether it is good for telling.'   Chris Smith

ISBN: 978-1-907359-39-2: 210 x 297mm
Ringbound: Paperback

Available Autumn 2014

History Stories for Primary School Children to Retell
Storytelling Schools Series, Volume III
Chris Smith and Adam Guillain

This is a unique collection of history-related stories, which can be learned and retold orally as a way of inspiring engagement and interest in history. The stories include commonly taught topics for primary school together with suggestions on ways to link the story to the teaching of history. The approach has been adjusted to fit with the 2014 primary national curriculum for England and Wales, and focuses mainly on British history from the end of the last ice age to the present day.

ISBN: 978-1-907359-44-6: 210 x 297mm
Ringbound; Paperback

Science Stories for Primary School Children to Retell
Storytelling Schools Series, Volume IV
Jules Pottle and Chris Smith

The authors have created a collection of stories for children to retell as a springboard for primary science teaching. Some of the stories have been created to contain the content of the science curriculum. Others are traditional stories that fit well with science topics and are great for oral retelling. The authors explain how to tell the stories, suggest ways of using them as a starting point for science teaching and also show how to link them to the teaching of literacy. Intended primarily as a resource for Storytelling Schools, this book will be of interest to all primary teachers who are looking for new ways to engage and inspire their classes about science.

ISBN 9789-1-907359-45-3: 210 x 297mm
Ringbound: Paperback

Future publications

A Storytelling Approach to Primary–Secondary Transition
Storytelling Schools Series, Volume V
Chris Smith and Nanette Stormont

A smooth transition between primary and secondary school is an important and often neglected part of the educational system. At a time of major change children work with uncertainty and fears of change as they move to their new schools. For some a difficult transition may lead to disengagement from secondary education.

In 2013 a group of storytelling primary schools in Oxford explored a way of using the Storytelling Schools approach to help children navigate this change. The basic idea was to use a single story, the *Odyssey*, to form a bridge between the two worlds: at the end of year 6 the students worked with the Cyclops story, using the Storytelling Schools methods and exploring issues of change, uncertainty and fear in the story and in relation to the move to a new school. Then at the beginning of year 7 students worked with the end of the story, *Return to Ithaca*, using a similar learning scheme. In

this way there was a sense of continuity and consistency between the two schools.

The authors have produced a step-by-step guide to adopting this model. While it is designed with Storytelling Schools in mind, it is a model which can be adapted for all primary–secondary transitions.

Model Primary Storytelling School Scheme
Storytelling Schools Series, Volume VI
Nanette Stormont and Chris Smith

The Storytelling School approach to education uses oral storytelling as a springboard for learning language, raising standards in writing and teaching in almost any topic of the primary curriculum.

This scheme provides a detailed example of a whole Storytelling School system, featuring:

➤ traditional and fiction stories for retelling

➤ sample plans for teaching narrative writing

➤ links to reading

➤ non-fiction topics and texts

➤ sample plans for teaching non-fiction using the storytelling approach

➤ sample plans for cross curricular links to other subjects

➤ tools for monitoring, evaluation and supervision

➤ communications materials for staff, students and parents to explain and support adoption of the approach.

It is intended as a reference for schools wishing to become Storytelling Schools, as a blueprint to be imitated and innovated as needed.

The Storytelling School, Early Years Handbook
Storytelling Schools Series, Volume VII
Chris Smith and Adam Guillain

Storytelling and storymaking are an integral feature of early years education, providing a crucial spur for child development in those first few years. Exposure to a rich storytelling environment builds language and social development in a natural and enjoyable way.

In this handbook the authors provide a step-by-step guide to developing storytelling in these settings, with guidelines for working with children from birth to 5 years. Areas include:

➤ ways of telling stories to children

➤ teaching the children to retell stories

➤ group storymaking and retelling

➤ the storytelling corner

➤ storymaking in free play

➤ storytelling and communication with babies and toddlers

➤ using chants and ritual to support the rhythm of the day

Stories, Chants and Rhymes for Early Years Children to Retell
Storytelling Schools Series, Volume VIII
Chris Smith and Adam Guillain

Every early years practitioner needs a repertoire of stories, songs, chants and rhymes so that they can create a rich story environment in their setting. In this volume the authors have collected a set of wonderful stories and rhymes that can be used to build the repertoire of every early years worker.

Index

A

additions (to story) 57
Anansi and the Tiger 55, 155
appreciation 5, 25, 27, 35, 42, 49
aspirational text 81, 84, 88
audio and video retelling 50
autonomy 6, 42, 58
avoiding anxiety 43

B

Baba Yaga's Black Geese 67, 87
basic plots 7 52–53, 54, 63, 64, 68, 69, 75, 96, 116, 122, 126, 150, 158
becoming a writer 77
believability 73, 74
Benjamin Franklin's Kite 142
Billy Goats Gruff 20, 21
biographies 72–73, 74, 75
boxing up diagram 110

C

cartoon strip 51
celebration and visibility 145, 148
changing stories 9, 57
characters 22
    basic 7, 52
    biographies 74
    dialogue 47
    invention from 66
    profile 48
    types 54, 56, 66
Cinderella 53, 63, 97, 101, 120, 139
classroom and corridor displays 149
choosing a story 11
cocktail party game 32
communal stories 20
comprehension 126
conversation and dialogue games 25, 32
Corbett, Pie iii, iv, vii, xiii, 3, 78, 81, 101, 104, 107, 122, 158
creative writing 3, 6, 81, 87

curriculum 2, 9, 35, 95, 149
    integration 115–144

D

dance/movement ix, 16–17, 21, 38–42, 51, 144, 149
deepening 1, 10, 46–57, 60, 66, 67, 78, 87, 95, 96, 107, 113, 124, 125, 126, 127, 140, 147, 149–151
dialogue 20, 25, 27, 32, 47, 48, 49, 57, 59
    games 25

E

eagles
    information about 109
empathy xiii, 4, 66, 133, 139
exercises 25–26

F

feedback 5, 19, 20, 27, 35, 36, 42–43, 44, 47, 49, 65, 66, 70, 72, 99, 113, 145, 148
feelings check–in 50
'fortunately/unfortunately' game 34, 62
Freedom Song 11, 12, 14–19, 21–24, 48, 60, 92, 101, 155
    deepening 47
    map 36
    plot matrix 58
    stepping 39, 41
    story 12–13
    with moods 24
Fu-Fu Bird 109–111

G

games
    cocktail party 32
    conversation and dialogue 32
    fortunately/unfortunately 34
    guessing 25, 26, 33
    passing around the circle 31

questioning 26
reflection and copying 30
role-play 32
show and tell with a twist 34
storymaking 34
who, what, where, when 30
'yes, let's'! 31
games and warm–ups 25–34
generate, reflect, select (learning triad) 78
geography 2, 6, 149
grammatical terms 79
Great Fire of London 128, 130
guide text 77, 79, 81, 83, 85

H

Hear, Map, Step, Speak (HMSS) 7, 11, 14–17,
    22, 35–37, 105, 113, 126, 132, 133
history 2, 6, 54, 74, 115, 117, 128, 132, 149, 157
how to teach a story 35–45

I

Icarus 134
imitation vii, ix–x, 7, 28, 30, 35, 57, 61, 98, 101,
    103, 104
imitation, innovation, invention (three 'i's) x, 7,
    28, 61, 109, 123
induction of new staff 145, 149, 151
innovation x–xi, 1, 7, 9, 23, 25, 28, 35, 41, 52,
        57–61, 78, 84, 98, 107, 147, 149, 150, 151
        76, 82, 98, 107, 108–125
inquisitiveness 6
invention x, 7, 9, 25, 28, 47, 52, 54, 57, 61–76, 96,
        98, 107, 109–125
        from basic plot 63
        from character 66
        using the plot matrix 6, 70
        what is 61
        with objects 69

J

Jub-Jub bird 103, 104, 106–108, 110

K

Key Stage 1 1, 77, 158
Key Stage 2 1, 158

L

language
    learning xiii, 2, 122
launching the policy 145–146
leadership 146
learning to tell 1, 36
listening skills 1, 4–5, 7, 20, 25, 32, 35, 36, 44
Little Red Hen 11, 20, 117, 139, 143
Little Red Riding Hood 30, 32–33, 44, 53, 57,
    83–86, 90–92, 101, 139

M

map 7, 11, 14, 23, 29, 35, 36, 37, 38, 41, 43, 47, 49,
    51, 52, 54, 143, 147, 148, 151
        Freedom Song 15
        with moods 24
        The Very Hungry Caterpillar 37
mapping ix, 20, 35–38, 43, 69, 73, 75, 97, 109,
    113, 124–5, 127, 132
memory xiii, 1, 2, 5, 6, 14, 17, 27, 36, 38, 41, 42,
    50, 63, 77, 104, 107, 147
mime 31, 33, 49, 51, 132
modelling 35, 65, 75, 77, 80, 81, 82, 102, 111, 113
Monkeys and Hats 20, 147, 156
Mother Goose of Oxford 68
music 9, 17, 18, 72, 76, 115, 144, 149

N

Nativity Chant 141
non-fiction x, 8, 54, 94–114, 118, 119, 121, 124,
    125, 128, 133, 143, 145, 147, 149, 151
        discussion 139
        exercises 99–100
        sequencing 103
        similarities and differences to fiction
        96–97

O

Otto Frank 129

P

paintings 50, 76
parents xii, 4, 7, 50, 100, 148, 145, 151
participative stories 9, 20–21
partnership funding 150
pictures 14, 17, 25, 29, 36, 47, 49, 51, 57, 59, 61, 74, 75, 76
playground mural 51
plot
    basic 1, 6, 7, 14, 17, 52–54, 63, 64, 65, 68, 69, 75, 97, 97, 116, 118, 122, 123, 124–126, 140
    matrix 22–23, 58, 62, 65, 70, 71, 79, 150
    recycling 55, 60
poems 45, 48, 49, 107, 127
poetry 127
policy
    language 8
    launching 145, 146–147
    whole school 149
PSE (Personal and Social Education) 133, 139, 140

R

radio/TV interview 50
rap 49
reading vii–x, xii, xiii, 1, 2, 5, 14, 50, 52, 53, 82, 104, 116
    integrating 126
re-enactment 25, 26, 33, 43, 48
repeating chants 21
refining a story 78
reflecting
    and copying games 30
    circle 27, 30, 31, 43, 51
    in small groups 31
religious education 2, 140, 149
response tasks 4, 20, 25, 35, 80

role-play 6, 32, 50, 86, 96, 98, 99, 100, 101, 107, 125

S

science 2, 6, 115, 142–3
screenplay 50
script 46, 50
shared creative writing and editing combined 81, 87
shared editing 80, 81, 82, 87
    examples 89–90
shared writing x, 8, 77–93
    examples 83–89
    key principles 77
    sessions 83
    'show don't tell' 90
    thinking like a writer 93
    tips 82
Snip–snip 11, 137, 155
speak xiii, 1, 5, 7, 10, 14, 17, 25, 26, 32, 35, 43, 47, 68, 94, 96, 99, 103, 105, 126, 127
staff
    induction (new staff) 8, 118, 145, 149
    teaching support staff 145, 148
step 38, 35
stepping 7, 16–17, 38, 41, 69, 79, 109, 132
    Freedom Song 16, 39
    theatre 42
    tips 41
    variants 42
stories
    changing 57
    choosing 11
    communal 20
    from everyday objects 28
    from pictures 29
    growing new 47
    how to prepare with HMSS 14
    participative 21
    planning into the curriculum 149
    tips for telling 18

types of, 20
story
    exhibition 51
    song 51
Story Museum iii, iv, xi, 11, 14, 17, 29, 54, 87, 118
    123, 133
storytellers ix, xiii, xv, 4, 5, 14, 46, 126, 149
storytelling
    assemblies 149
    benefits 3
    'starters' 25
Storytelling Schools 1–10, 145
    becoming a Storytelling School 145, 151
    building up skills 145
subject
    areas 8
    learning 6
substitution 59
support
    networks 150
    staff 148

T

teaching support staff 145, 148
'tell me more (lies)' 25, 28, 32, 68
'tell me more (truth)' 25, 26–28
telling stories 17–19
    at home 51
    independent 5, 21
    tips 18
    thought corridor 49
term plans 124–125
thinking–feeling–choosing 140
Three Dolls xiv
truth and story 140
types of stories 20
    communal 20

U

unilateral demonstration modelling 82

V

Very Hungry Caterpillar 37, 40, 53

W

warm-ups 9, 25–34, 62, 99, 100, 101, 103
word-for-word oral imitation 104–105
writing
    independent 10, 77, 109, 113, 124
    shared x, 8, 9, 10, 77, 81, 109
    shared creative writing and editing 81
    ways to demonstrate 81

Other Books from Hawthorn Press

The Storyteller's Way
A Sourcebook for Inspired Storytelling
Sue Hollingsworth, Ashley Ramsden

Everyone can tell a story, but to tell it well you need a certain set of skills. Whether you're starting out or want to develop your storytelling expertise, this book is an essential guide.

Use it to tell stories for entertainment, teaching, coaching, healing or making meaning. It contains a wealth of stories, exercises, questions, tips and insights to guide your storytelling path, offering time-tested and trusted ways to improve your skills, overcome blocks and become a confident and inspirational storyteller.

ISBN: 978-1-907359-19-4; 228 × 186mm; paperback

Storytelling with Children
Nancy Mellon

Telling stories awakens wonder and creates special occasions with children, whether it is bedtime, around the fire or on rainy days. Encouraging you to spin golden tales, Nancy Mellon shows how you can become a confident storyteller and enrich your family with the power of story. Find the tale you want from Nancy's rich story-cupboard.

Nancy Mellon runs a School for Therapeutic Storytelling and lives in New Hampshire

ISBN: 978-1-903458-08-2; 216 × 138mm; paperback

The Natural Storyteller
Wildlife Tales for Telling
Georgiana Keable

In these pages you will find over fifty nature stories, chosen to bring both teller and listener closer to their environment. These culturally diverse stories that have stood the test of time will engage young readers, and encourage them to become natural storytellers. The stories are accompanied by tips on telling, story maps, riddles and practical activities.

The Natural Storyteller recently won first place in the Green Books/ Environmental category of the *Purple Dragon ly Book Awards*.

ISBN: 978-1-907359-80-4; 228 x 186mm; paperback

Therapeutic Storytelling
101 Healing Stories for Children

Susan Perrow

This treasury of healing stories addresses a range of issues – from unruly behaviour to grieving, anxiety, lack of confidence, bullying, teasing, nightmares, intolerance, inappropriate talk, toileting, bedwetting and much more. The stories also have the potential for nurturing positive values.

Susan Perrow M.Ed runs therapeutic storytelling workshops from China to Africa, Europe to America and across her own sun-burnt land of Australia.

ISBN: 978-1-907359-15-6; 234 × 159mm; paperback

Advent and Christmas Stories

Estelle Bryer and Janni Nicol

From Advent and the Twelve Days of Christmas, to the flight into Egypt: Estelle Bryer and Janni Nicol tell their favourite Advent and Christmas stories. Their approach is simple yet profound and draws on their lifelong experience as Waldorf kindergarten educators, puppeteers, and as mothers. These stories will delight young children, and invite parents and teachers to become more confident storytellers.

'Will help make Christmas a magical time for children'
Sally Jenkinson, author, The Genius of Play
ISBN: 978-1-907359-25-5; 228 × 186mm; paperback

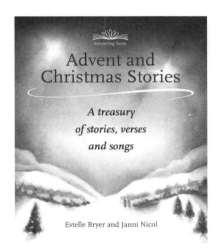

An A-Z Collection of Behaviour Tales
From Angry Ant to Zestless Zebra

Susan Perrow

Telling the right story at the right time can help children face challenges and change behaviour. Particularly relevant for children aged three to nine years, all 42 stories begin with an undesirable or out-of-balance situation, then, through metaphor and an imaginative story journey, they lead to a more desirable resolution. A pencil drawing accompanies each story.

Susan Perrow specialises in storytelling and creative discipline. She travels internationally giving workshops and training seminars.

ISBN: 978-1907359-86-6; 234 x 156mm; paperback

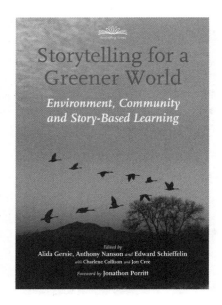

Storytelling for a Greener World
Environment, Community and Story-Based Learning
Alida Gersie, Anthony Nanson and Edward Schieffeliin
Foreword by Jonathon Porritt

This unique sourcebook promotes environmental mindfulness and sustainable behaviour in adults and children.

Written by 21 cutting-edge professionals in the field of story-based learning and pro-environmental change, this treasury of 47 stories details many creative activities and descriptions of inspiring practice for both newcomers and seasoned practitioners.

ISBN: 978-1-907359-35-4; 234 x 159 mm; paperback

Healing Storytelling
The Art of Imagination and Storytelling for Personal Growth
Nancy Mellon

Nancy Mellon shows how to create a magical atmosphere for the telling of tales, how to use movement and direction within a story, how to set a storyscape, beginnings and endings, how to best use the rhythms of voice. Here are also the more subtle ingredients of storytelling including moods, the elements, seasons and the symbolism of magic words, objects and weapons which represent the external and archetypal forces in our world.

ISBN: 978-1-912480-13-5; 234 x 156mm; paperback

Hawthorn Press

www.hawthornpress.com

Ordering Books

If you have difficulties ordering Hawthorn Press books from a bookshop, you can order direct from our website **www.hawthornpress.com**, or from our UK distributor **BookSource**: 50 Cambuslang Road, Glasgow, G32 8NB Tel: (0845) 370 0063, E-mail: orders@booksource.net. Details of our overseas distributors are on our website.